The Finance of Health Care

The Finance of Health Care

Wellness and Innovative Approaches to Employee Medical Insurance

Murray Sabrin

BEP
BUSINESS EXPERT PRESS
Leader in applied, concise business books

The Finance of Health Care:
Wellness and Innovative Approaches to Employee Medical Insurance

Cover design by Charlene Kronstedt

Interior design by Exeter Premedia Services Private Ltd., Chennai, India

First published in 2022 by
Business Expert Press, LLC
222 East 46th Street, New York, NY 10017
www.businessexpertpress.com

ISBN-13: 978-1-63742-405-6 (paperback)
ISBN-13: 978-1-63742-406-3 (e-book)

Business Expert Press Healthcare Management Collection

First edition: 2022

10 9 8 7 6 5 4 3 2 1

Description

Employers Can Reduce Their Employees' Health Care Costs by Thinking Out of The Box

Employee health care costs have skyrocketed, especially for small business owners. But employers have options that medical entrepreneurs have crafted to provide all businesses with plans to improve their employees' wellness and reduce their costs. Thus, the cost of employee health care benefits can be reduced markedly by choosing one of numerous alternatives to traditional indemnity policies.

The Finance of Health Care provides business decision makers with the information they need to match the optimal health care plan with the culture of their workforce. *This book is a must guide* for corporate executives and entrepreneurs who want to attract—and keep—the best employees in our competitive economy.

Keywords

wellness; medical care; health/medical insurance; employer-based insurance; transparency; medical care alternatives; universal medical care; single-payer system

Contents

List of Figures

Testimonials

"If you are an entrepreneur or an employee, if you are a retiree or the chairperson of a major corporation, if you feel that you understand your health plan or are clueless, if BCBS, ERISA, ACA, PPO, HMO CDHP, FSA, are meaningless 'BS,' if you need to reduce your escalating medical insurance costs or are trapped in a financial maze, Dr. Sabrin's The Finance of Health Care, *is the most important book that you will ever read. It will enable you to successfully navigate the health insurance options. It will give you an insight into wellness as an essential part of the medical insurance package. If you want to anticipate and benefit from the major improvements in health care coverage that are underway, buy it and pass it on to your friends, business associates, insurance agents, educators, policymakers and doctors. America will forever thank you."*—**Dwight Carey, serial entrepreneur for over 60 years involved with over 200 start-ups, Professor of Entrepreneurship and Engineering, Temple University**

"When entropy sets in, and economic systems decline in their capacity to deliver quality outputs to customers, reform is not the answer. Creative ingenuity in system design and redesign is required. It takes a special mind and a creative approach, to shift from the constrained thinking of the economics of scarcity to the open-ended possibilities of the economics of abundance. Medical insurance is a glaring example of a system in decline, and Murray Sabrin is the economist for our time, demonstrating and defining the new and eminently practical pathways that will lead us to a better system for provisioning and paying for medical care."—**Hunter Hastings, economist and venture capitalist, Economics for Business, hunterhastings.com**

Acknowledgments

I would like to thank Paul Mladjenovic who recommended me to Business Experts Press acquisitions editor Ed Stone, who navigated the proposal for this book to a successful conclusion. Ed's professionalism was evident from the birth of the book idea to throughout the evaluation process. I appreciate the valuable feedback that improved the manuscript from the following individuals: Charles Bens, Charles Frohman, Glenn Gero, Hunter Hastings, Kishore Jethanandani, Jared Wallen, and Wayne Winegarden. I would also like to thank BEP managing editor Scott Isenberg for his wise input, Charlene Kronstedt for guiding the manuscript through the production process, and the team at Exeter for their editorial support, which shaped the manuscript for publication. Any omissions or other shortcomings of the book are the author's responsibility.

Introduction

Why has medical insurance become so expensive—and complicated? Once upon a time, patients were "cash customers" for most of their medical expenses. A patient would see a doctor and pay—usually a him—five dollars for the office visit, and if the ailment were serious enough to require a prescription, the medicine could be purchased for a few dollars at a local pharmacy. I know from my own experience growing up in New York during the 1950s and early 1960s. That's what my parents paid to have their children diagnosed and treated. There were no co-pays, no deductibles, and no insurance claim forms to fill out. And when my blue-collar father needed a hernia operation in April 1961, his employer-based insurance, Blue Cross/Blue Shield, paid the bills. I don't remember if there were any out-of-pocket expenses my parents paid to either the surgeon, anesthesiologist, or Lenox Hill hospital where the surgery was performed. If my parents had to pay any expenses not covered by insurance, it was not onerous because I don't remember them complaining that the medical bills were going to "wipe" out their savings.

As price inflation began to accelerate in the mid-1960s and reached double digits in the early and late 1970s and early 1980s, medical care inflation became the fastest rising component of the Consumer Price Index. Not coincidentally, the passage of both Medicare and Medicaid in 1965 fueled the demand for medical care. And with the federal government making generous funds available to get hospitals and doctors to get on board with both programs, the flow of money in the medical sector increased substantially. Over time, employers saw the premiums of their traditional medical insurance polices supplied by the big insurance companies increase dramatically. In some years, premiums increased by double-digit rates when other prices increased marginally. American employers faced a major financial crisis.

Nevertheless, medical insurance, in short, has become as "American as baseball, hot dogs, and cherry pie." Less than 10 percent of Americans do not have medical insurance coverage, even though the Affordable Care

Act (ACA), also known as Obamacare, was supposed to get the uninsured coverage because it provided generous subsidies.

How can employers navigate the medical insurance maze and offer their employees a benefit that would achieve several objectives: improve their health, provide them with access to competent primary physicians and specialists, and pay for hospital and other coverage for a major illness or chronic conditions? This is the challenge for employers.

While traditional medical insurance costs at an all-time high, employers do have options to achieve the above objectives and improve their bottom line. From self-funding medical insurance to offering Health Savings Accounts, Health Reimbursement Accounts, and other plans to give employees greater choices to address their medical care needs, medical entrepreneurship is indeed providing alternatives for employers and their workforces.

Instead of being "passive" purchasers of medical insurance, employers will find the information and resources they need to reduce one of the highest costs they face. With price inflation reaching a 40-year high recently, it is imperative for entrepreneurs to learn how they can keep their medical care benefits under control in what may be another period of relatively high inflation.

For business decision makers, the information provided in several chapters is reliable, but the usual caveat applies. Check with your tax advisers and other professionals—insurance brokers, for example—regarding the latest government rules that may affect any changes to your medical benefits.

CHAPTER 1

The Workforce, Wellness, and Healthy Outcomes

How healthy are American adults? According to one metric, 42 percent of adults are obese,[1] up from 30 percent 20 years ago.[2] This may increase to 50 percent by 2030.[3] Thus, based on the relationship between weight and wellness, a substantial number of Americans can reduce their incidence of debilitating illnesses such as type 2 diabetes, hypertension, cancer, heart failure, stroke, and other chronic ailments by shedding excess pounds. Overweight, obesity, and other unhealthy conditions are some of the factors that have propelled the nation's medical care bill to $4 trillion (about $12,000 per person in the United States) in 2021.[4]

Moreover, a survey by the American Psychological Association revealed that more than 40 percent of American adults had undesirable weight gains during the COVID-19 pandemic, averaging 29 more pounds. The survey also revealed that 61 percent of Americans had gained weight during the COVID lockdowns and when working remotely. In addition, 10 percent of respondents reported they gained more than 50 pounds. Alcohol consumption also increased as stress, anxiety, and lack of access to gyms for months caused "emotional eating."[5]

In short, the unintended consequences of lockdowns and other policies that have caused stress, anxiety, and frustration, which led to more food and alcohol consumption than otherwise would have occurred absent the pandemic, will probably lead to greater increases in chronic illnesses in the future. The country's medical bill will undoubtedly increase markedly if the weight gains by tens of millions of Americans cause the number of adults to succumb to type 2 diabetes, hypertension, heart disease, cancer, and other life-threatening diseases in the next several years.

This would create a great challenge to businesses that pay for traditional medical insurance to cover their employees, the self-employed who must obtain insurance coverage in the private marketplace, and the federal government, which picks up the tab for tens of millions of retirees (Medicare) and eligible low-income families under Medicaid. States pick up some of the costs of the more than $800 billion Medicaid outlays (about $1,800 per person in the United States). Retirees may also see their Part B (traditional Medicare) or Part C (Medicare Advantage) premiums increase as well. Both cover physicians' bills, medical tests, and other nonhospital medical expenses.

Against this backdrop, we need to differentiate the different types of medical issues individuals face and the tactics and strategies employers have used to keep their employees healthy. This begs the question whether employers should be responsible for their employees' well-being. According to Charles Bens, PhD (nutrition), a wellness consultant to companies wrote who wrote in an e-mail to me (February 27, 2022), "Owners and CEOs who do not pay serious attention to wellness are actually contributing to the health care crisis and impeding the ability of America businesses to compete in the world marketplace. This should be a requirement written into every CEO's contract, as well as all of the performance agreements of every manager in every company." Bens also suggests that companies "should promote profit sharing as a means of getting employees to appreciate the importance of wellness to the bottom line."

Nevertheless, employers have taken on the responsibility by providing medical insurance for their employees, presumably to assist employees pay for their medical bills. And to keep insurance premiums from eating away at companies' revenues and ultimately profitability, employers have been taking on a much greater role providing employees with opportunities to obtain optimal wellness.

Wellness, Sickness, and Disease

Although most people would consider themselves well if they are not sick nor have a disease, there are degrees of optimal wellness, according to Dr. Glenn Gero, a New Jersey-based naturopath, who explained optimal wellness in a telephone interview (September 18, 2021).

An individual's wellness can be undermined by imbalances in the body, such as high blood pressure and ailments not discovered in most conventional blood tests. In addition, wellness may also be a "psychological" or self-esteem issue. Recently, a 35-year-old former college football player who weighed 345 pounds came to see Gero, because he wanted to lose weight. Gero ordered a series of blood tests and they all came back negative; the patient's lungs and heart were "normal," even though he had 40 percent body fat. To help him lose weight, Gero recommended a dietary modification as the first step to the patient losing weight. The patient never returned for a follow-up visit.[6]

There are at least two takeaways with the episode of an overweight former football player who was seeking professional advice on how to shed his excess pounds. One, a relatively young overweight individual may not have any underlying physical disorders, at least for the time being. That's the good news. Two, Dr. Gero assessed the young men's physical condition and recommended a course of action to help him lose weight. Unless Dr. Gero hears from individual in the future he will never know if his patient will have achieved his goal. Dr. Gero's interaction with this young man confirms the old adage, "you can lead a horse to water but you cannot make him drink." Another obvious conclusion from this brief vignette is that individuals are ultimately responsible for their health care.

Illness and Disease

Human beings suffer from common colds, sore throats, earaches, upset stomachs, or some other illness during the year that prevents them from having an optimal health. In other words, people get sick from dozens of non-life-threatening illnesses and usually recover in a short period of time. The good news is that our immune system can fight off many of these illnesses, or an over-the-counter remedy can nick the malady in the bud. And for many folks, Grandma may have some homespun solution in her "medicine chest" that she has used for decades to combat a common illness without having to see a physician. For some hardy individuals, a minor illness would not prevent them from going to work. Assuming that an illness is not contagious, you must admire people "who will tough it out" instead of staying home to get back to "normal." Employers tend to admire individuals so to speak who step up to the plate and do not allow a minor illness preventing them from going to work. Employees tend to receive recognition from their companies for not missing work, and we have all heard stories about postal workers, teachers, police officers, and fire-fighters, who have never missed a day at work in 20, 30, or even 40 years or more. A remarkable achievement that deserves our admiration and respect.

A disease, on the other hand, is a chronic condition that causes a "malfunction" of our bodies that can last for years and maybe life-threatening. Type 2 diabetes, cancer, congestive heart failure, lupus, sickle cell anemia, and scores of other debilitating diseases require accurate diagnoses and appropriate protocols that would allow an individual to function in and out of the workplace to the best of his or her ability. Diseases, therefore, are expensive to treat and both employers and employees have an incentive to make wellness a major priority in the workplace. This leads to the obvious question: what can employers do or should do to improve the wellness of their employees? In addition, what is the responsibility of employees to maintain their health so they would avoid high rates of absenteeism and remain a productive member of the workforce? These questions need to be addressed so medical care costs can be reined in to prevent skyrocketing medical insurance rates.

Incentives for Optimal Health

Individual choices may account for 40 percent of premature deaths in the developed world. It is common knowledge that smoking, eating unhealthy foods, and sitting on the couch too much tend to shorten life spans.[7] Public officials have addressed lifestyle choices and health outcomes with taxes on alcohol and tobacco products to discourage consumption and introduced information campaigns to persuade the public to discard unhealthy choices. Clearly, with national governments around the globe paying for a substantial portion of medical care costs with single-payer systems such as in Canada and the UK, policy makers have been attempting to keep a lid on medical costs (no government has an unlimited medical care budget!) and help improve their citizens' health with numerous incentives.

But what about employers? Employers have several options to improve the well-being of their employees. One approach employers have implemented—personalized incentives—is based on a simple proposition: what is important for employees to improve their health and maintain a life of optimal well-being?[8] Financial incentives for weight loss and reducing A1C scores (for diabetics) by using mobile apps so employees can monitor their progress have shown success in improving employees' well-being. Other incentives include so-called socially motivated goal setting as a member of a team or on an individual basis. These activities include weekly steps, gym attendance, and other measures to burn off calories.[9]

A possibly more compelling reason for employees to improve their well-being can be described as "intrinsic incentives." In this case, one's health is a reward in and of itself. Physicians play a crucial role helping an individual set goals while employees would monitor their progress through various feedback loops. Thus, research reveals that incentives not only promote healthy outcomes in the workplace but also change behavior in the general population, as long as the program is well structured.[10]

There are numerous workplace wellness programs that have proven to be effective that employers should consider. Selecting one that fits the company's workplace "culture" is critical to its success. Dr. Steve Aldana, CEO of WellSteps, compiled a list of wellness programs from 15 companies and from the applicants to the C. Everett Koop Health Project. The Health Project was created 25 years ago to award companies that improve employee well-being and reduce costs associated with medical care. Aldana's essay lists 18 incentive ideas from Koop award applicants, ranging from cash awards to discount employee health insurance premiums, gift cards, raffles, contributions to health reimbursement accounts, and drawings for search items as iPads, travel vouchers, fitness equipment, and so on. In addition, Aldana summarizes 15 incentive strategies from unidentified companies that were submitted in the Koop Award competition.[11] At the end of the essay, Aldana provides links to commonly asked questions about wellness programs and the workplace.

According to nutritionist Charles Bens, PhD, founder and president of Health at Work, Inc., author of nine books, including *Healthy at Work: Your Pocket Guide to Good Health*, who has presented his wellness ideas to scores of employers around the globe, there are several factors to optimal health (www.drcharlesbens.com). In an e-mail to me (February 6, 2022), he outlined the following perspectives and insights.

1. Weight loss is one key factor; however, nutritional status is more important. Over 90 percent of the adult population has nutritional deficiencies based on studies from the National Cancer Institute, North Carolina University, and Stanford Medical School.
2. The recommended dietary allowance (RDA) standards are wrong and represent minimal nutritional needs. The United States Department of Agriculture (USDA) standards are not much better and the national school lunch program is a joke.
3. About 70 percent of U.S. adults are overweight and 97 percent of weight loss programs fail according to the national registry on weight gain.
4. A vast majority of employers use punitive measures to lower health care costs such as higher deductibles, higher co-pays, and reduced coverage. This actually makes employees less well in the long term.
5. Over 95 percent of employers who have a wellness program do not have a written wellness plan with measurable goals and objectives.
6. The allopathic medicine (commonly called conventional, Western, or orthodox medicine taught in medical schools) is used by a vast majority of doctors to treat symptoms with standardized medications and surgeries without regard to the root cause of the problem. Chronic illness represents over 80 percent of health care costs and should be treated with functional medicine protocols (applying "natural" remedies, such as herbs, plant-based remedies, and other protocols), which are safer, more effective, and much less costly.
7. There is only good science to support 20–25 percent of what allopathic medicine does. Functional medicine has good science for about 80–90 percent of what they do and they treat the root cause and the whole body with personalized integrative medicine. This medicine combines the evidence from allopathic and function medicines.

8. A vast majority of doctors and hospitals are using the wrong diagnostic models and tools. The A1C is not the best test for diabetes. Mammography is not the best diagnostic tool for breast cancer. Cholesterol is not the best test for heart disease. And statin drugs cause more harm than good. I have the science to support all of this.

9. The problem (in wellness programs) is that the organizational culture is wrong. Wellness should be a cultural priority and embedded in the company's business plan. Employers should combine expanse reduction in operations and health care to create a profit-sharing program. That gets attention and results. My clients prove this.

For employers that want to achieve two major goals—keeping their employees healthy and reducing medical care costs—Bens's website would be an excellent starting point to implement a wellness program. A well-structured wellness program would reduce absenteeism, improve productivity, and probably increase morale. A healthier workforce also reduces medical insurance premiums, which would increase the bottom line, and free up resources for additional investment. In addition, employers whose medical insurance costs decline and productivity increases would be in a position to increase wages and salaries of employees— another huge benefit to a successful wellness program.[12]

Nevertheless, there are caveats regarding a wellness program that employers need to be aware of. One review of wellness programs points out that a poorly designed program may, in fact, encourage unhealthy behavior. As bizarre as that possibility may seem, focusing on individual behavior rather than just the "workforce" could help reluctant employees who may feel stigmatized or shamed because of their health status to participate in a wellness program.[13]

Managing Incentives

Assuming an employer is committed to a wellness program because of increased absenteeism, declining productivity, rising medical insurance premiums, or poor quality control, managing the incentives becomes a challenge. The challenges are multidimensional. With more and more employees working remotely, the lack of personal interaction in the workplace probably requires different strategies and incentives to improve and maintain a healthy workforce. Wellsteps.com provides numerous recommendations that employers could review, such as dealing with remote workers, how to improve the health of blue-collar workers, and how to implement mindfulness in the workplace, to name a few.[14]

Dr. Aldana analyzes why corporate health and wellness programs fail in an extensive essay published on his website.[15] The key takeaways from his overview can be summed up as follows: (1) some wellness programs just hold the events and do not track employee participation; (2) programs are too complicated to monitor; (3) applying sticks and carrots; (4) not bringing a wellness expert to work with employees; (5) providing the wrong incentives, which do not leave to permanent behaviors; (6) using a wellness portal instead of a wellness program, expecting employees to be self-motivated; (7) not including spouses and significant others when designing the wellness program; (8) a wellness committee is essential for a successful program, including employee representatives; (9) not integrating a wellness program into the corporate structure; and (10) treating a wellness program as a benefit instead of a perk (which tends to be fleeting) has a greater chance of success.

The challenge for corporate managers and even small business owners is to design a wellness program that is cost-effective, provides the appropriate incentives, and can track improvements in employees' health and behavior. Short-term health benefits that dissipate over time may, in effect, be counterproductive, especially if an employee's weight loss causes him or her to put back the pounds and more after the incentives are ended. This phenomenon can be observed as well in smoke cessation programs and for excessive alcohol treatments. Initially, success may give way to previous unhealthy lifestyles. And with the COVID pandemic still in the minds of many individuals and polls showing that the American people are concerned about staying healthy more so than any time in recent history, "selling" a wellness program should be the proverbial "no-brainer" to employees.

Behavioral changes may be easy or hard depending on the motivation of employees who enroll in a wellness program. Managing the incentives successfully, in the final analysis, would provide a substantial return on investments as outlined above. Corporate managers thus must determine if any financial incentives undermine intrinsic incentives—a question that is not easily answered before a wellness program is enacted. A personalized approach to wellness seems to have the greatest opportunity to achieve the goals of both employers and employees.

Diet, Exercise, and Healthy Outcomes

When the COVID lockdowns began in March 2020, Andrew Hurst's essay, "Americans Aren't Doing Enough to Stay Healthy," highlights some of major health issues facing the American people.[16] He cites a survey by ValuePenguin, which was conducted at the end of February and March 2020, which reveals how Americans' habits would increase risks to their health and possibly the community at large. For example, 42 percent of the respondents indicated they don't wash their hands after using the restroom; insufficient sleep for many people may compromise their immune systems; more than 50 percent of Americans do not get an annual physical, and when they do they may be less than truthful about their health; going to work sick would be okay for more than 25 percent of Gen Xers and millennials and one-third of Gen Z; and more than 20 percent of people have been untruthful to their employers or insurer about their health.[17]

Since the survey was taken, media reports about COVID hospitalizations and deaths and public health officials and others emphasizing washing your hands frequently, getting enough sleep, and practicing good overall personal hygiene most likely has had a substantial impact on people's habits.[18] In addition, the survey reported that one-third of Americans are eating enough vegetables weekly and only 30 percent exercise regularly. Nearly half of smokers want to quit and about 10 percent of respondents want to reduce their sugar intake. The key findings reveal what public health officials, physicians, and health care writers have known for a long time—the American people in general need to end so-called bad habits to improve their overall health.

Federal Government Food Plate

The federal government's *Dietary Guidelines for Americans, 2020–2025*, which provides "the core elements that make up a healthy dietary pattern," was first published in 1980.[19] The purpose of the publication is "for policy makers and nutrition and health professionals to help all individuals and their families consume a healthy, nutritionally adequate diet"[20] and to help prevent disease. Clearly, worthwhile goals were to reduce chronic illnesses, to keep the American people healthy, and help keep medical care costs under control.

The *Dietary Guidelines* focus on eating sufficient vegetables and fruits, grains, fat-free or low-fat dairy products, protein-based foods such as lean meats, and eggs, beans, and nuts. Restricting sugar, saturated fats, sodium, and alcoholic beverages appear on every list of "dietary dont's."[21] The *Dietary Guidelines* recommendations are virtually identical to the "Healthy Eating Plate" (HEP) published by the Harvard Medical School.[22] In addition, the HEP recommends staying active, for the obvious reasons, burning off calories is an important component of weight control. Although one of the common food groups—whole grains—which most dieticians and other health care providers would consider noncontroversial, there are some physicians and naturopaths who would take exception to the recommendation that about a quarter of the food we eat should come from carbohydrates. According to Dr. Bens, "People need 7–9 helpings of vegetable and fruits daily. Five still promotes disease." In addition, is a low-fat diet based on sound nutritional evidence? We will explore this in the next section about alternatives to conventional diet recommendations.

Alternatives to Conventional Diets

A "diet" is not a short-term fix to a health issue. Healthy eating is not a diet, but a lifestyle that provides adequate nutrition, helps ward off chronic illnesses, bolsters an individual's immune system, and maintains a person's "normal" body weight. These are the goals medical care professionals, dieticians and nutritionists, and health care writers would agree on. The devil is always in the details.

In January 2020, WebMD reported on the U.S. News and World Report ranking the best diets. The Mediterranean diet topped overall best list for the third year in a row.[23] Hallie Gould's essay "10 Popular Diets That Actually Work" also cites the Mediterranean diet as number one on her list. A Mediterranean diet is based on consuming ample portions of "vegetables, olive oil, fish and chicken" and avoiding "processed foods, salt, red meat and saturated fat."[24] For wine lovers, red wine is permissible in the Mediterranean diet. According to one nutritionist quoted in the article, "it's [the Mediterranean diet] preventive medicine at its finest."[25] Other diets on the list include 5:2 Diet, the Paleo Diet, the Alkaline Diet, WW (Weight Watchers), and several more. This essay would be a good first step for individuals to learn about healthy eating to improve their health and avoid chronic illnesses. As Hippocrates observed centuries ago, "Let food be thy medicine and medicine be thy food."

Neurologist Dr. David Perlmutter has promoted another perspective about wellness and healthy eating that challenges the conventional diet where whole grains should be about 25 percent of food consumed by adults. The author of such books as *Grain Brain, The Grain Brain Cookbook, Brain Maker,* and several others, Perlmutter presents the science as he asserts on his "Low-Carb" blog:

> Adopting a much lower carbohydrate diet while welcoming healthful fat back to the table is a top-notch approach for achieving better blood sugar control as well as weight loss. To be sure, this is a diet that shouldn't exclude carbs that contain dietary fiber, which is so important for the health of our gut microbes.[26]

Perlmutter's website, drperlmutteer.com, contains numerous essays about healthy eating to avoid chronic illnesses that he believes can be prevented by following Hippocrates' 2,500-year insight.

When it comes to embracing a medical professional's suggestions, it is imperative to read critically the recommendations and discuss them with your family physician and others in your professional and personal network. As the website makes clear in on the home page: "You Control Your Health Destiny."

Benefits of Exercise

Keep moving. Obviously, not all the time, but enough time of the day to stay flexible, keep your circulation going, and burn off some calories. Working remotely since the pandemic began in March 2020 has led to substantial weight gain among adults and youngsters have been deprived of gym classes and other activities that are essential to their well-being, not the least of which is their mental health. So, if you are wondering what you can do to stay in shape, Jen Murphy describes four routines anyone can do at home without needing any special equipment.[27] Many of these exercises are what we did in gym class or in a gym with a personal trainer. Now you can stay in shape and save money by doing it yourself! Even only 30 minutes of exercise would provide substantial benefits to remote workers or anyone else who wants to stay in shape, especially residents of parts of the country where late fall and winter preclude some individuals (many) from walking or exercising outdoors. For businesses, making these exercise templates available to their employees would be a costless way to help them improve their well-being and reduce absenteeism.

In *The Mental Health Benefits of Exercise,* an overlooked activity to increase well-being is the need to exercise to combat depression, anxiety, stress, improve memory and thinking, improve sleep, and build resilience.[28] The bottom line is Hippocrates' insight about food should be amended to include exercise as a modern kind of "medicine." And let's not forget that "laughter is the best medicine."[29]

The biochemical reaction of laughter in the human body has proven to be a wonderful tonic to improve well-being. Watching a classic movie comedy or sharing jokes with friends and colleagues (in this day and age, joke telling can get you in trouble in the workplace, especially if one that has a religious, ethnic, gender, or racial overtone) releases endorphins that make us feel better. So if you are feeling "down," grab that joke book and have a good belly laugh. Or watch one of the funniest movies in the past six decades with an all-star cast, "It's a Mad, Mad, Mad, Mad World."[30]

Conclusion

Who is responsible for the American people's well-being? The question should not be too difficult to answer. Every adult oversees his or her eating habits, exercise routine, and other factors that affect an individual's both short- and long-term health. Thus, it is the responsibility of individuals to obtain the information to improve their well-being and be productive members of the workforce. The information provided above is the starting point for young adults to begin a lifelong journey of health and well-being and for middle-aged Americans to improve their well-being and to avoid chronic illnesses as they age.

Employers could play an important role in having a healthy workforce, which would lead to greater productivity, less absenteeism, and lower medical costs, and ultimately higher profits. A well-structured wellness plan, of which there are many, avoids the pitfalls of introducing a program that was not well thought out. Employers have access to resources outlined in this chapter that would reap benefits to them and their employees. Thus, the well-being of the American people will be determined by how much responsibility they take for their health care and how well employers facilitate their employees' well-being. If all the so-called pieces fall into place, the American people will be healthier than they otherwise would be. Both employers and employees have a vested interest in having not only a safe workplace but also a healthy workforce. Together, they can achieve a healthier workforce for decades to come.

CHAPTER 2

Medical Care

A History

Aren't you glad you live in the 21st century rather than the 17th, 18th, or 19th century when medical care was so primitive that a minor ailment often meant an early—and certain—death? And if you were fortunate to survive childbirth and infancy, some of the best medical treatments were home remedies that treated several illnesses. Although the practice of medicine can be traced to the Greeks and Romans, it wasn't until the major breakthroughs in the late 19th and early 20th centuries that infants, children, and adults were able to survive because of the discovery of life-saving drugs and vaccines. Prior to these life-altering medicines and therapeutics, for most human beings, life was short and sometimes painful.

The great advances in medicine, hygiene, and nutrition have boosted life expectancy from just 40 years in 1860 to nearly 79 years in 2020. Since 2014, life expectancy has declined marginally in America; the major factors for this phenomenon are attributed to poor diets, a sedentary instead of an active lifestyle, rising medical costs, and increased rates of suicide.[1] In addition, drug use has curtailed the lives of many young adults and other demographic groups who have suffered from depression and other mental illnesses, especially during the first wave of the COVID-19 epidemic. Nevertheless, the survival rate for many "death sentence" diseases, such as cancer and other chronic conditions have improved markedly in the 21st century. In addition, the survival rate for COVID-19 is more than 99+ percent for most of the population. For the elderly (age 65+) in general, the COVID-19 death rate was 93 per 100,000, which varies widely by state depending on the vaccination rate.[2] Which begs the question, what were the underlying health conditions of the individuals who died from COVID-19?

Undoubtedly, a COVID-19 type of pandemic in the 18th or 19th century would have caused a substantial portion of the population to die. Although the death toll from COVID-19 reached 955,000 by the early 2022 out of a US population of 332 million (less than 0.29 percent mortality rate), assuming, of course, the death count is accurate and does not merely indicate individuals who died *with* COVID instead of from COVID, surviving this alleged virulent illness in America today is very high.[3]

How has medical care evolved since the time when getting sick meant only at best a 50–50 chance of survival? Today, we have seen enormous success in contemporary medical practices and the saving of millions of lives. Let's look back at the earliest days of the practice of medicine to learn how knowledge has been discovered, which has led to the enormous increase in life expectancy.

Early Physician Care

In colonial America, the practice of medicine can be divided into two components—rural medicine and urban treatment. In rural areas where physicians were few and far between, home remedies were used to deal with typical medical problems. Occasionally, a physician would visit a rural resident and pull out a rotten tooth after which the individual would be in substantial pain. Payments were usually made in kind—food, other agricultural products as well as such items as handkerchiefs. Follow-up visits were weeks and months in the future, if at all.[4] Meanwhile, as America urbanized in the early part of the 18th century, physicians and patients had more frequent contacts. Physicians typically kept detailed records of their visits, the ailment being treated and payment received, leaving a treasure trove of data regarding the practice of medicine in colonial America.

Cotton Tufts, a Harvard-educated physician, in the late 18th century treated fevers as well as stomach and throat illnesses with "a solution of wine and lemon juice, salt, loaf sugar and distilled cordial water served in a wine glass." In short, American physicians used "natural" treatments, a reflection of the influence of the Caribbean trade routes. Scholars concluded colonial physicians also relied on the expertise of Native Americans' knowledge of indigenous plants and herbs to treat patients.[5]

Even in the 1700s physicians disparaged women midwives and local healers who did not have formal medical training and lobbied to have New Jersey, for example, establish "professional medical standards" to prevent "quackery." These efforts, in effect, limited the supply of doctors "to white male physicians trained in European-influence schools of thought."[6]

Undoubtedly, the outbreak of smallpox was the earliest medical challenge to the colonists during the American Revolution and the early years of the fledgling American republic. George Washington who contracted smallpox in 1751 on the island of Barbados had acquired immunity. When the American Revolution began, the disease was ravaging his troops in their battle for independence. Washington made the decision after consulting with his physician advisors to inoculate his troops with the virus so they would be protected from a full-fledged illness. It worked. The contagion was contained, and as they say the rest is history. America became an independent nation.[7]

Prior to 1820 medical training primarily consisted of apprenticeships. Soon proprietary medical school founded typically operating independently of a university or hospital. Licenses were usually not required to practice medicine and a reaction to the more or less unregulated medical marketplace doctors formed the American Medical Association (AMA) in 1847. Ostensibly, the purpose of the AMA was to establish high standards for medical doctors and impose sound clinical principles in the practice of medicine.[8]

Not surprisingly, the Civil War would have a major impact on the practice of medicine. With large numbers of soldiers huddled closely together, disease transmission became a major concern. This concern prompted the establishment of public health boards and more research into infectious diseases. The casualties on the battlefield led to Civil War surgeons returning home with new techniques to treat residents.[9]

This era could be classified as the "professionalization" of medical care. State licensing of physicians became more common, medical specializations increased, and with it associations of doctors who no longer would be considered general practitioners. And government funding of medical facilities began modestly.[10]

The Modern Age: Remedies and Quacks

The modern age of medicine began on the eve of the Civil War, when at least 55,000 physicians were practicing, making the United States "one of the highest *per capita* number of doctors in the world (about 175 per 100,000)." A decade later, the number of physicians jumped to roughly 62,000. Most physicians were conventional doctors but some were homeopaths (approximately 5,300) and less than 3,000 were eclectics, who treated patients with herbs and other noninvasive therapies.[11] The battle was on for the establishment of best practice medical protocols, which would have ramifications for the evolution of medicine. In addition, the path that medicine took more than 150 years ago would set the agenda for federal and state legislation, the costs of medical care, and ultimately the effects on the doctor–patient relationship.

Like many myths about episodes in American history, economist Dale Steinreich challenges the conventional wisdom that some early medical practices were based on "snake oil" salesmen traveling from town to town with their ineffective or worse poisonous "remedies" duping a suspecting public. Steinreich emphasizes this is a myth perpetrated by moviemakers who based their portrayals on the medical establishment's assertion that conventional medicine is sound, even though early treatments such as bloodletting and the use of metals were killing patients. The real reason, according to Steinreich, that conventional medicine practitioners (allopaths) were adamantly opposed to both homeopaths and eclectics, is that they cut into the allopaths' incomes.

Soon the AMA began to push for legislation that would reduce the number of medical schools and hence the supply of doctors. In some states, the AMA would call for the outright ban of homeopaths and eclectics, which would further reduce the supply of medical practitioners. And to add insult to injury, in 1870, the AMA prohibited women and blacks from joining the organization.[12]

The most ominous development in the history of medical care was the notorious Flexner Report, named after Abraham Flexner, brother of Simon Flexner, a director of the Rockefeller Institute for Medical Research. In short, the Flexner Report, a product of the Carnegie Foundation, was essentially the AMA's Council on Medical Education (formed in 1904) 1906 report that recommend the closing of many medical schools, which declined from 166 at the time to 77 during World War II. Rural medical schools were closed in great numbers and only two Black medical schools were allowed to remain open. Not surprising, the law of supply and demand worked its magic, physicians' incomes rose dramatically as the supply of new doctors were curtailed markedly.[13]

Good news for physicians but bad news for the American people. Government intervention in medicine has driven up prices for patients under the guise of "protecting" the public from unscrupulous nonconventional practitioners, who may not have attended AMA- and state-approved medical schools. This is another example of "regulatory capture," where one interest group uses the power of the state to squelch competition and drive up prices.

The Committee on the Costs of Medical Care (CCMC) was created (1925) and funded by the Carnegie Corporation, other private foundations, with assistance from the AMA, the American Hospital Association, government agencies, and think tanks to address medical price inflation. In 1932 the CMCC published a comprehensive report based on previous studies, asserting the increase in medical care costs were somehow the result of new technologies and other scientific breakthroughs as well as greater utilization of hospitals, and increased costs of medical training and supplies. However, restrictions of the supply of physicians is the primary culprit in the medical price inflation that began when policies enacted by state governments at the behest of the Flexner Report became widespread.[14]

As the supply of doctors was restricted so too was the supply of hospitals. For-profit hospitals felt the sting of burdensome regulations and had to play on an unleveled playing field in competition with nonprofit hospitals, which did not have to pay income or property taxes. Furthermore, government subsidies and tax-deductible contributions gave nonprofit hospitals the financial edge over their for-profit counterparts. In the 1920s, 60 percent of all hospitals were for-profit, and that percentage dwindled to 11 percent by the late 1960s.[15] However, for-profits comprised nearly 25 percent of all hospitals in 2019.

Community Self-Help Groups

Legendary investor Warren Buffett, who has been CEO of Berkshire Hathaway since 1965, once quipped something to the effect "there are two types of competition I don't like—foreign and domestic."[16] Competition tends to lower prices for consumers as producers have to make sure they are providing *value* for their customers; otherwise, they will patronize a competitor who is providing a better value. It is no different in the professions. Competition among practitioners means consumers can shop for the highest quality, low-cost provider. The history of self-help organizations is yet another example of attempts to squash competition and thus drive up prices for consumers.

As David T. Beito recounts in his history of mutual aid organizations, fraternal societies provided affordable medical services to their members during the late 19th and early 20th centuries. A local lodge would hire a physician who was a salaried employee of the fraternal society. Members of the lodge were enthusiastic about having access to quality, low-cost medical care. One of the criticisms from the medical profession was the under-cutting of prevailing fees by fraternal societies.[17]

The concept of contract practice dates to the colonial when plantation owners hired doctors to treat slaves. This practice continued in many industries after the Civil War. Labor unions used contract practice to provide medical care for miners. In New Orleans Black mutual aid societies hired physicians to treat their members on a per capita basis. In the early part of the 20th century, the lodge practice was making inroads in Chicago and New York and was mainly popular among Italians, Greeks, and Jews.[18]

In New York City, for example, dispensaries were created and provided low-cost medical care. Doctors who worked in dispensary were volunteers or donated most of their time for free. New Orleans had a robust tradition of fraternal societies providing medical care to members. Some of these organizations were founded well before the Civil War. A major impetus for the creation of mutual aid societies in New Orleans was the need to protect people from the vicissitudes of life and the dearth of government's social welfare spending. Nevertheless, the lodge practice thrived for many decades because doctors were typically "on call" for members.[19]

The lodge practice peaked in the 1920s after the medical profession "launched an all-out war." In many states, medical societies sanctioned physicians who entered into lodge contracts. In addition, county societies were actively undermining lodge practice.[20] The relentless assault on a community solution for low-income families reveals how using the power of the state and cartel-like arrangements in medical care reduced the availability of physician services. This is yet another reminder of the adage that some have called an enduring myth, "we are from the government and here to help you."

Employer-Based Medical Insurance

The earliest example of employer-based medical insurance occurred in Oregon and Washington in the early 1900s, when companies began to cover the medical costs of their timber and mining workers. To keep costs down, adjusters scrutinized the fees and procedures as well as hospital stays of injured workers. Physicians resented someone looking over their shoulders regarding their practice of medicine.

Meanwhile, as hospitals expanded, they needed a consistent income stream to pay for their fixed costs. To address this financial issue and to help employees pay for hospital costs, Dallas schoolteachers, in 1929, negotiated a contract with Baylor University Hospital for hospital insurance. Teachers paid six dollars per year in premiums; in return they would receive up to 21 days of hospital care. Soon, this idea spread and became the basis for Blue Cross, which began operations in Sacramento, California, three years later.

During the Great Depression, physicians were concerned about getting paid for their services because of the high unemployment gripping the nation and the rise of compulsory national health insurance plans. Physicians were also worried that with the rise of prepaid plans like Blue Cross, their fees could be curtailed if employers embraced a similar medical care model hospital for other third-party payers. To counteract these threats, physicians created Blue Shield (the first one began operations in 1939) as way to get paid for the services in the bleakest economic period in American history. I will discuss both Blue Cross and Blue Shield in-depth in Chapter 3.

The great leap forward in employer-based medical insurance occurred during World War II when the federal government-imposed wage-price controls to dampen the inflationary pressures of the Federal Reserve's easy money policies and military spending. Employers were prevented from raising wages and offered tax-free fringe benefits like medical insurance to attract workers. The die was cast—employees now expected business to provide health insurance as part of their compensation package.

A clarification is in order. Comprehensive "health insurance" is in effect the responsibility of every adult, who has a personal obligation to himself or herself to lead a healthy lifestyle to prevent virtually all illnesses. However, we know that there are diseases that run in families—cancer, heart disease, diabetes, and so on—and therefore have to be addressed throughout one's lifetime. Medical insurance, on the other hand, is, therefore, necessary to pay for so-called big-ticket medical procedures that are out of the financial reach of the average employee. Pooling resources via insurance or any other method to reduce the financial risk for major medical illness is both prudent and wise. But medical insurance has evolved into a prepaid plan for virtually all medical costs, a distortion of the primary principle of insurance, which is to cover unexpected, catastrophic expenses, not usual and common doctor visits and procedures.

Employer-based medical insurance thus is another example of the law of unintended consequences. Employers never envisioned before World War II that they would be responsible for their employees' medical insurance. In short, the federal government's economic policies were the spur for this arrangement. Financially sound employee compensation packages would focus on wages and salaries and employees would then allocate their incomes for retirement savings and medical care costs, including catastrophic insurance. Of course, employers could provide their employees with vendors who would make their "pitch" to them so they could make wise choices regarding their individual/family needs. I will review the medical insurance markets in Chapter 4 and how they evolved in Chapter 5.

CHAPTER 3

The Blues® to the Rescue?

Two of the most iconic symbols in America are associated with the Blue Cross and Blue Shield (BCBS) companies. This should not be surprising because the Blues® provide medical coverage for one in three Americans, about 111 million people. The BCBS companies cover nearly three-quarters of America's Fortune 100 employers, including Microsoft, Walmart, General Motors, and UPS. Small business employers provide coverage for 6.8 million employees. An additional 17 million Americans are covered by BCBS companies, which include retirees and their families as well as unionized workers. The Federal Employee Health Benefits Program provides coverage for 5.8 million federal workers, retirees, and their families. Finally, the Blues® provide Medigap supplemental insurance, Medicaid coverage, Medicare Advantage plans, and Medicare Part D drug plans, covering 16 million Americans.[1]

Individuals can obtain coverage from the Blues® through the Affordable Care Act or through the Office of Personnel Management multi-state plan.[2]

BCBS companies provide coverage in every U.S. zip code, processed more than $510 billion in annual claims, and have contracts with more than 1.7 million doctors and hospitals. Additional facts reveal the scope of the Blues® reach across America. The companies spent nearly $12 billion to deal with the COVID-19 epidemic, funded community health programs ($367 million), and employees volunteered 581,000 hours to local projects and social initiatives and also donated $15 million for local causes. The companies provided nearly $2.5 million for disaster relief efforts.[3]

The BCBS Fact Sheet asserts in the section about health care and innovation:

> Blue Cross and Blue Shield companies believe our healthcare system should deliver safe, high-quality care; eliminate inefficient

spending; and encourage and reward actions that individuals take to improve their health. *Through innovative programs, the Blue System is improving care delivery and collaborating with physicians and nurses to help them choose evidence-based medical treatments that will best meet the unique needs of each patient.*[4] (Emphasis added)

The emphasized statement above reflects sound medical practices—treating each patient based on his or her specific needs rather than a one-size-fits-all approach. The implications for what should seem like an obvious best medical practice for any society can be applied to so-called public health issues like COVID-19. Although public health issues are outside the focus of this book, employers nevertheless should be sensitive to the needs of their employees when government mandates have been issued. As we have seen in Chapter 1, a healthy workforce is a win–win for employers and their employees. The employer-based medical insurance structure in place for the vast majority of workers would best serve employees if medical care decisions would be made with input from all the stakeholders in the workplace, but in the final analysis left to the doctor–patient relationship. That would be a transparent and honest discussion of medical decisions and protocols by employers, employees, and insurance representatives.

How did one company, in reality a federation of 35 independent and locally operated BCBS companies, become the largest provider of health care coverage whose reach is felt in every community across America?

I will explore the history, operations, and benefits/costs of the BCBS companies below so employers would have an overview of the insurance behemoth to help guide them in making an informed decision about coverage for their employees.

History of Blue Cross and Blue Shield

The stock market crash of October 1929 and the subsequent economic contraction that became known as the Great Depression had widespread immediate financial repercussions for virtually all institutions and organizations. Hospitals felt the money crunch as revenues declined when individuals postponed/delayed getting treated because of lower incomes as the unemployment rate rose markedly beginning in 1929. To increase its cash flow, Baylor University Hospital in Dallas (1929) contracted with schoolteachers to provide a maximum of 21 days in the hospital for $6 per year. That's right! For 50 cents per month, the 1,500 teachers would have their hospital bills paid at a time when patients were rarely hospitalized for that length of time.[5] This idea rapidly spread to other hospitals. Although the Baylor Plan was called insurance, it was more like a prepaid plan for services.

Insurance historically was used to protect against unforeseen catastrophic losses. The Baylor Plan, on the other hand, was not insurance as it was typically understood and soon became the "model" for health insurance throughout the country. However, as more and more hospitals adopted some version of the Baylor Plan, it set the stage for "economic dislocations" in the medical field. Treatments that could be done on an outpatient basis were now being done in hospitals, where the expense is much greater. Furthermore, in a typical indemnification policy, the insurance company would pay the insured for the loss, who would then "shop around" to obtain the best possible care and price. The prepaid plans made patients insensitive to medical care prices, because the plan would pay the hospital directly.[6]

Not surprisingly, the medical profession supported this arrangement, because steady cash flows from the new insurance plans kept their incomes relatively stable during the Great Depression.

Nevertheless, the American Hospital Association (AHA) organized the hospitals that adopted the Baylor Plan, which became known as Blue Cross, but not without some bumps in the road, less than patient-friendly policies, and the special privileges Blue Cross obtained from state and federal governments.[7]

One of the AHA's goals was to keep medical prices high. To achieve this objective, hospitals in the Blue Cross system allowed subscribers to choose their physicians but limited their hospital choices to ones in the BC system. Although "choice" was central within the system, single hospital plans were omitted as a choice.

As the Blue Cross system was established, state insurance regulators wanted to oversee the hospitals and have them set aside reserves as other insurance companies had to do. Instead, the hospitals argued their "reserves" are the hospitals themselves and all the resources at their disposal, doctors, nurses, and others as well as the medical equipment. The states accepted this argument. Blue Cross hospitals became nonprofit and tax-exempt institutions, not subject to insurance regulations.[8] For these special privileges, Blue Cross accepted anyone even those with preconditions and offered charity care as part of their community mission.

The Blue Cross business model had a major component that reflects its powerful position. As John Steele Gordon explains, "… hospitals came to be paid almost always on a cost-plus basis, receiving the cost of services provided plus a percentage to cover the costs of invested capital. *Any incentive to be efficient and reduce costs vanished.*"[9] (Emphasis added) In short, hospitals in the Blue Cross system as well as other hospitals that have insurance companies pay for their subscribers' hospitalization do not base their "prices" on *value their "customers" receive* but on their costs and a markup. Thus, the disconnect between patients and the value they receive in hospitals, in effect, was cemented in American medical care with the creation of Blue Cross.

Blue Shield

The 1930s were a challenging time for physicians. The unemployment rate stayed well above 10 percent during the decade, taking its toll on the incomes of physicians. Physicians were weary of being paid by a third party, such as an insurance company, which they believed would lower their incomes even further during the depression. Advocates of national health insurance wanted President Roosevelt to include a compulsory health insurance plan in the Social Security Bill, which he eventually signed in August 1935. Strenuous opposition from the medical establishment killed the national health insurance plan in the Social Security legislation.[10]

With the popularity of Blue Cross, physicians were warming up to the idea of prepaid plans for their services. The concern was how these plans were to be structured. The American Medical Association (AMA) adopted a set of principles in 1934 that physicians would essentially be in control of prepaid plans, including the right to set prices based on the ability of patients to pay.[11]

Formally, Blue Shield began operations in 1946, seven years after the California physicians service created a plan where employees who earned less than $3,000 annually were eligible to join for a fee of $1.70 per month. Blue Shield plans also received the same enabling legislation that allowed it to become a tax-exempt organization and they were not subject to insurance regulations. The plans provided benefits for hospitalized members while some plans also covered doctors' visits. Blue Shield would reimburse subscribers who, in turn, would pay physicians the difference between the doctors' bills and the amount reimbursed. This "mixed indemnity" plan allowed physicians to retain control over their pricing power.[12]

As both Blue Cross and Blue Shield evolved and the demands for employer-based health insurance became popular with workers and labor unions in the post–World War II booming economy, the two blues merged in 1982 and became known as the Blue Cross and Blue Shield Association.[13]

Operations

The merger of Blue Cross and Blue Shield 40 years ago created the largest American health insurance company, in reality, an association of state companies, serving thousands of corporations and small businesses. And with both Medicare and Medicaid requiring additional administrative support to handle the claims of tens of millions of beneficiaries, the Blues® have, in their words, innovated and "leading the way toward a future where data empowers patients."[14]

According to the blog entry, shared data among physicians creating an "interoperable" health care system is necessary for information to be accessed by both doctors and patients to improve patient care.[15]

Examples of this commitment to an interoperable health care system include Anthem Blue Cross Blue Shield using medical records and health insurance claims to predict where there are member health care gaps and risks, especially among the elderly who are vulnerable to falls. Regence has worked with Apple so its members have a better experience using the tech giant's health app. In addition, it has worked with Pacific Northwest health care systems to help members retrieve their health data more easily so they can reduce pre-authorization wait times and manage medication needs more efficiently. Florida Blue members can access their records through a third-party application to better coordinate "their health care journey." And in Michigan, the BCBS is involved in an initiative to create a Health Information Exchange (HIE), which would share data with doctors in the expectation that better decisions would be made to improve members' health. Real-time alerts are being delivered to physicians and other medical personnel about high-risk patients to reduce "unnecessary hospital admission."[16]

BCBS acknowledges that employer plans should be customized for a variety of reasons. Thus, what one network solution may be appropriate for one small or medium-sized business may not work for other similar-sized businesses. BCBS offers four network solutions that may be able to be customized for the employer. The next step would be to obtain all the specific benefits and costs for each of the network solutions that your state BCBS offers to make an informed choice if you decide to go this route. (See www.bcbs.com/employers#tailoring.)

BCBS's Total Care mission is to partner "with doctors and hospitals nationwide to improve health outcome for … employees and curb the rising cost of healthcare." Recently, BCBS evaluated claims comparing the Total Care provider to non-Total Care ones and found a more than 30 percent reduction in health care costs.[17] What is Total Care that achieved such stunning results? As BCBS explains:

> Total Care is the nation's largest network value-based programs—accountable care organizations (ACOs) and patient-centered medical homes (PCMHs)—that reward quality of care instead of quantity. Participating providers are focused on better care coordination, chronic condition management, prevention and wellness to help your employees stay healthy and out of the hospital.[18]

According to the BCBS website, the total care approach is providing "a better healthcare experience and quality-of-life for employees." This is based on a January 2018 evaluation that reveals that total care performing better 22 out of 23 key measures nationally.[19] Benefits managers have to do their due diligence to unpack the assertions made by BCBS on its website. Doing so could save your company as much as 30 percent in medical insurance premiums.

Insurance companies are in a competitive environment and employers are more cost-conscious than ever regarding employee fringe benefits. Every 10 percent reduction in medical insurance premiums goes right to your company's bottom line. If BCBS can reduce your company's insurance costs *and help improve your employees' well-being* at the same time, then a huge win–win will ensue, resulting in less absenteeism, higher productivity, and greater morale.

BCBS Benefits

Employee well-being has become many companies' ongoing strategy to reduce medical insurance premiums. As was pointed out in Chapter 1, several strategies could improve employees' health, be relatively inexpensive, and long-lasting. Nothing is more frustrating than short-term success and long-term failure. What does BCBS's plans offer employers who want to improve their employees' health for the foreseeable future?

As a new resident of Sunshine state, I accessed the Florida Blue website to review their benefits package for employers. Each state BCBS is an independent entity; employers therefore would have to review their state's Blue plans to determine which benefits are most attractive and cost effective for their company.

The Florida Blue Employers page summarizes its health plans and their benefits, which are published at www.floridablue.com/employers/plans-services/health-insurance.

Health Plans and Programs

Virtually all health care professionals would agree that everyone deserves quality health care that's affordable. Florida Blue, for example, provides value health solutions that meet a broad range of needs. According to Florida Blue, "Regardless of whether your focus is on providing your employees with 'high value' benefits and choice or on the providing the lowest priced alternative available, we've got you covered. Our end-to-end approach to care and wellness, including focus on prevention and personal guidance, ensure excellent outcomes for your employees and real demonstrated value for your business." Florida Blue offers comprehensive benefits to its members as outlined on its website, www.floridablue.com/employer/plans-services/health-insurance. A sample of the benefits include in and out-of-network coverage, cost-sharing options, integrated tax-advantaged accounts such as Health Savings Accounts, Flexible Spending Accounts or Health Reimbursement Accounts, preventive care, prescription coverage, wellness and education programs, and personalized coaching, and other benefits to improve employees' well-being.

Florida Blue also offers high-deductible plans that when coupled with a Health Savings Account (HSA) may be more beneficial for employees than a traditional insurance policy. Again, due diligence is necessary to sort out the strengths and weaknesses of such an insurance arrangement for your employees. HSAs will be discussed in Chapter 5 along with other Health Reimbursement Accounts and Flexible Savings Accounts.

Blue Cross and Blue Shield claims the local Blues® are providing cutting-edge insurance services to one-third of Americans by integrating technology with patient-focused health care. Shouldn't medical care always have been and be patient-centric?

CHAPTER 4

The Rise of the Medical Insurance Market

What we commonly call health insurance can be traced to the creation of hospital associations in the latter part of the 19th century. Railroads built hospitals in unsettled areas to treat their workers who became sick or injured on the job. Similarly, logging, coal, and metal mining companies built hospitals and hired doctors to give their workers the medical care they needed because of serious injuries they suffered in these hazardous businesses. Employees paid for the medical care with a fixed payment deducted from their pay. This fee structure became the forerunner of managed care.[1]

Meanwhile, at the beginning of the 20th century, a period known as the Progressive Era, workers' compensation insurance programs were established (1910–1915) in 32 states to protect employees when they were injured on the job and to provide employers with legal protection from onerous lawsuits. The medical establishment typically supported this legislation, believing that employees would seek medical care from their family physician. However, companies began to hire doctors to treat their employees, reducing the demand for independent family doctors—and thus their incomes.[2]

Although commercial insurance had existed well before the prepaid medical plans were created in the late 19th and early 20th centuries, health insurance was generally considered uninsurable. Eventually, commercial insurers entered the health insurance market with hospital coverage in the 1930s. These indemnity policies paid the insured an agreed amount to cover part or all of their hospital surgery, alleviating the worry of physicians who were concerned that insurance companies would contract with selected hospitals and physicians.[3]

As prepaid group plans were becoming more common in Los Angeles, Elk Grove, Oklahoma, Milwaukee, Chicago, Washington DC, Seattle, and other cities, the Kaiser Foundation Health Plan in California (1933) ruffled doctors' feathers. The Kaiser Plan built its own hospital to serve its members whose doctors were denied access to nonparticipating hospitals. A series of lawsuits by the Justice Department and prepaid plans to allow all physicians admitting privileges in local hospitals was making inroads.[4] Hospitals could no longer deny physicians who were treating prepaid members' access to their facilities.

Medical insurance got a huge shot in the arm when President Roosevelt imposed wage and price controls during World War II. Employers could no longer raise wages and salaries to attract workers, but instead provided employees with a tax-free medical insurance benefit. From about 9.1 million Americans with private health insurance in 1940, that figure rose to 82.9 million in 1975. In 2020 the best estimate of private health insurance coverage was 66.5 percent of all Americans, or approximately 216 million, who had medical insurance.[5]

Medical insurance became enormously popular with employees, especially unionized private and public sector workers who had another form of compensation to negotiate at the bargaining table.

While employer-based insurance was expanding throughout the postwar period, the calls for more government involvement in medical care were gaining steam but did not go anywhere until 1965 when President Johnson signed legislation creating Medicare (for seniors) and Medicaid (for low-income Americans) as part of his Great Society program. The bipartisan support for both programs makes them "untouchable" for the time being, especially with Medicare having nearly 60 million enrollees and Medicaid paying the bills for nearly 58 million Americans.[6]

In 1974, the Employee Retirement Income Security Act (ERISA) was passed by Congress to shore up employer-defined benefit pension plans with the creation of the Pension Benefit Guarantee Corporation (PBGC). In addition, employer self-insured medical plans were becoming popular because companies paid premiums administered by an insurance company based on "experience" rating. This meant that companies used their own claims experience to fund the plans, thus avoiding an insurers' community rating approach, which tended to raise its premiums. A self-insured plan would be less costly to administer because high-speed mainframe computers lowered the cost of information processing. As the fledgling technology lowered prices, third-party administrators entered the marketplace to process these claims.[7]

During the price spirals of the 1970s and early 1980s, the cost of medical care was the fastest rising component of the Consumer Price Index. It still tends to be. To deal early on with medical price inflation, health maintenance organizations (HMOs) were created based on the earlier prepaid plans. Soon other managed care plans, PPOs (preferred provider organization) and POS (point of service) plans were introduced as additional managed care plans to give employees more choices in obtaining medical care.[8]

By 2020, PPOs covered 47 percent of workers up from 11 percent in 1988. HDHP/SO plans (a high deductible/savings option plan) covered 31 percent of workers as compared to 8 percent in 2008. HMOs have been declining in popularity, covering 30 percent of workers in 1998 to 8 percent in 2020, and POS plans also have become less in demand, falling from 22 percent in 1998 to 8 percent in 2020.[9]

On the cost front, the average annual worker premium for family health insurance rose from $13,770 in 2010 to $17,545 in 2015, to $21,342 in 2020, while an employee's share of the insurance premium increased from $3,997 (2010) to $4,955 (2015) to $5,558 (2020), contributing 27 percent of the total premium cost. Although the premium increase was 27 percent for the five years ending in 2015, it still increased a hefty 22 percent for the five years ending in 2020.[10] Although employer-sponsored health insurance premium increases have decelerated markedly from the 1990s and early 2000s, the actual outlays have not declined but increased at a slower rate[11] (see Figure 4.1). This is the good news. However, the issue for both employers and employees is obvious: are they getting *value* for their premium dollars? This is a theme I will examine as we review, in future chapters, alternatives to the most popular managed care plans, which were supposed to dampen insurance premium hikes.

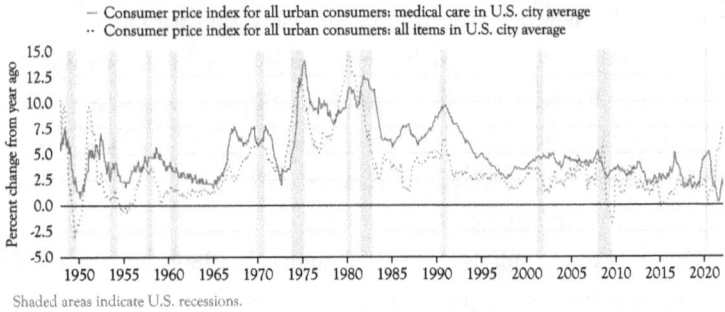

Figure 4.1 Annual percent rate of change in medical care versus the CPI

Source: U.S. Bureau of Labor Statistics, Consumer Price Index for All Urban Consumers: Medical Care in US City Average [CPIMEDSL], retrieved from FRED, Federal Reserve Bank of St. Louis; https://fred.stlouisfed.org/series/CPIMEDSL, March 29, 2022.

Government Regulations

Government regulation of health insurance began modestly in the early years of employer-based insurance. During the Progressive Era, when economic regulation took a giant leap forward, the incremental steps that led to substantial oversight and intervention of health insurance reflected the shift from a relatively laissez faire economy in the 19th century to the interventionist state in the 20th and 21st centuries.[12] As Mike Holly points out, "Since the early 1900s, medical special interests have been lobbying politicians to reduce competition. By the 1980s, the U.S. was restricting the supply of physicians, hospitals, insurance and pharmaceuticals, while subsidizing demand."[13] In addition, Holly cites the following laws and policies that have restricted the supply of medical care facilities and physicians that have contributed to medical price inflation for the past several decades (see "How Government Regulations Made Healthcare So Expensive," https://mises.org/wire/how-government-regulations-made-healthcare-so-expensive).

- In 1910, the physician oligopoly was started during the Republican administration of William Taft after the American Medical Association (AMA) lobbied the states to strengthen the regulation of medical licensure and allow their state AMA offices to oversee the closure or merger of nearly half of medical schools and also the reduction of class sizes. The states have been subsidizing the education of the number of doctors recommended by the AMA.

- In 1925, prescription drug monopolies begun after the federal government led by Republican president Calvin Coolidge started allowing the patenting of drugs. (Drug monopolies have also been promoted by government research and development subsidies targeted to favored pharmaceutical companies.)
- In 1945, buyer monopolization begun after the McCarran–Ferguson Act led by the Roosevelt administration exempted the business of medical insurance from most federal regulation, including antitrust laws. (States have also more recently contributed to the monopolization by requiring health care plans to meet standards for coverage.)
- In 1946, institutional provider monopolization begun after favored hospitals received federal subsidies (matching grants and loans) provided under the Hospital Survey and Construction Act passed during the Truman administration. (States have also been exempting nonprofit hospitals from antitrust laws.)
- In 1951, employers started to become the dominant third-party insurance buyer during the Truman administration after the Internal Revenue Service declared group premiums tax-deductible.
- In 1965, nationalization was started with a government buyer monopoly after the Johnson administration led the passage of Medicare and Medicaid, which provided health insurance for the elderly and poor, respectively.
- In 1972, institutional provider monopolization was strengthened after the Nixon administration started restricting the supply of hospitals by requiring federal certificate-of-need for the construction of medical facilities.

- In 1974, buyer monopolization was strengthened during the Nixon administration after the Employee Retirement Income Security Act exempted employee health benefit plans offered by large employers (e.g., HMOs) from state regulations and lawsuits (e.g., brought by people denied coverage).
- In 1984, prescription drug monopolies were strengthened during the Reagan administration after the Drug Price Competition and Patent Term Restoration Act permitted the extension of patents beyond 20 years. (The government has also allowed pharmaceutical companies to bribe physicians to prescribe more expensive drugs.)
- In 2003, prescription drug monopolies were strengthened during the Bush administration after the Medicare Prescription Drug, Improvement, and Modernization Act provided subsidies to the elderly for drugs.
- In 2014, nationalization will be strengthened after the Patient Protection and Affordable Care Act of 2010 ("Obamacare") provided mandates, subsidies and insurance exchanges, and the expansion of Medicaid.

Reproduced with permission of the Ludwig von Mises Institute.

It is no coincidence that medical care prices "took off" in the 1960s with the passage of Medicare and Medicaid coupled with the Federal Reserve's easy money policies to fund President Johnson's Great Society programs and to finance the Vietnam War (Figure 4.2). Easy money policies since the 1960s have propelled virtually all prices upward. Occasionally, the Fed's tight money policies to cool off an overheated economy have not interrupted medical care inflation. The recent low medical price inflation during the pandemic of 2020–21 may have been more due to less demand for elective surgery and postponing medical care than any structural changes in the health care sector. Nevertheless, controlling health care costs has been a top priority of businesses.

— Consumer price index for all urban consumers: medical care in U.S. city average
··· Consumer price index for all urban consumers: all items in U.S. city average

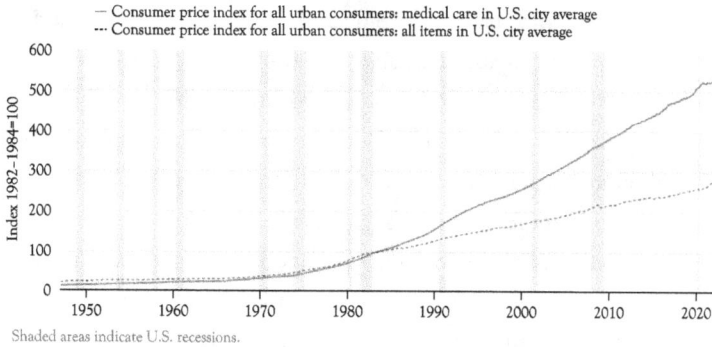

Shaded areas indicate U.S. recessions.

Figure 4.2 Long-term trend of medical care inflation versus the CPI

Source: US Bureau of Labor Statistics, Consumer Price Index for All Urban Consumers: Medical Care in US City Average [CPIMEDSL], retrieved from FRED, Federal Reserve Bank of St. Louis; https://fred.stlouisfed.org/series/CPIMEDSL, March 29, 2022.

To help keep costs down for the public, President Trump signed the No Surprises Act at the end of 2020, which is designed to protect consumers from surprise medical bills, beginning January 1, 2022. As the cost of medical care has outpaced most workers' wage and salaries, families have been grappling with spiraling medical bills, especially for emergency services. Other provisions of the bill include "health plans must cover surprise bills at in-network rates; balance billing is prohibited; out-of-network providers cannot send patients bills for excess charges and specific oversight and enforcement activities are required."[14]

Although this law would prevent families from getting a huge medical bill that could be financially devastating, the law only addresses one aspect of the nation's expensive annual medical care costs. In the next section, we will examine the major insurance companies' missions and how they are addressing the cost issues employers and individuals face in the marketplace.

Major Health Insurance Companies

In the previous chapter, we reviewed the history and structure of the "Blues®," the largest insurance provider in the country. Blue Cross and Blue Shield companies are part of the acronym, BUCHA, the Blues, United Healthcare, Cigna, Humana, and Aetna, which collectively cover the medical insurance needs of the overwhelming number of Americans or are major players in administering employers' self-insured plans.

United Healthcare (UHC) has 330,000 worldwide employees who provided 2.6 million hours of voluntary service. The company made $47 million in charitable contributions and had revenues of $257 billion in 2020. In *Fortune* magazine's list of the World's Most Admired Companies, UHC was ranked number one in insurance and managed care. The UHC website contains substantial information, including the company's structure, its mission, and information about the health plans it offers and just about everything you need to know about one of the most successful health insurance providers in the marketplace. For employers and individuals, the most valuable pages are devoted to "Improving Health Care Affordability."

United Healthcare has several initiatives to achieve its goals sections improving cost transparency, implementing value-based care "by providing actionable data and care management tools that deliver better outcomes at a lower cost to consumers, governments and the health system."[15] The creation of Accountable Care Organizations (ACO) is to assist "groups of health care providers that work together to coordinate patient care [and] provide higher quality care at a lower cost." Patients who are members of an ACO "are more likely to see a primary care provider, get preventive screenings and avoid eye hospital admission or visit to the emergency department (ED)."

United Healthcare projects by 2030 that "more than 55 percent of outpatient surgeries and radiology services among our members will be delivered at high-quality, cost-efficient sites of care ..." Accordingly, UHC estimates if more joint replacement surgeries were done in ambulatory surgery centers, there would be 500,000 fewer hospitalizations and savings of $3 billion annually. In addition, diagnostic testing done at the doctor's office or stand-alone imaging center instead of an outpatient hospital department would reduce costs by 62 percent and save patients $300 per test.

United is lowering prescription drugs by using point-of-sale discounts through OptumRx, which also provides a drug discount card program for all Americans that can be used at more than 64,000 pharmacies.

Cigna

Cigna traces its roots to 1792 when the Insurance Company of North America (INA) was formed in Philadelphia. In 1912 Connecticut General (CG) was created to offer accident insurance and seven years later began to offer group accident and sickness contracts. In 1982 the two companies merged into what is now Cigna, and in 1998 began to focus on health care almost exclusively.[16]

To choose a health care provider for your business is no easy task. Cigna gives six reasons to choose it: (1) controlling costs and improving quality, (2) bundled services help keep costs lower, (3) improving health through wellness, (4) personalized 24/7 customer engagement, (5) clinical quality and innovation, and (6) increase engagement and boost employee health.[17]

In the competition for workers in a relatively tight labor market, as during the "Great Resignation," employers need to concentrate on cost containment as well as focusing on providing consumer value. And with health care expenses still a line item that has a marked influence on a business' bottom line, employers need to evaluate Cigna's maze, so to speak, of medical insurance options that will deliver value to you as an employer and provide your employees with quality care to meet their health care needs. Cigna offers traditional insurance plans and self-funding options that may be a good fit for your business.[18] Examining Cigna's options with the Blues, UNH and the two other companies I will discuss next would be a useful exercise to structure a plan that would be the most cost-effective in this competitive environment.

Humana

Humana's mission is to the point "… to help achieve lifelong wellbeing" by offering health plans for businesses from 2–99 employees and 100 plus employees.[19] Most plans have a wellness component, virtual doctor visits, preventive care, and pharmaceutical benefits. Humana has a page for employers to peruse a matrix of Humana's plans to see which is the best fit for their companies.[20] This is a worthwhile page to review, because employers can have at their fingertips an overview of Humana's plans in an easy-to-read format. Like the insurance providers above, Humana stresses affordability, a much sought-after goal of employers. Humana also provides studies to reinforce a concern for employers, maintaining a healthy workforce.[21]

If employers want to consider a self-funding option, links on the Small and Large Group Insurance page will lead them to the information they need to make an informed decision.

Aetna

Aetna began selling life insurance in 1850 and in 1899 entered the health insurance market. Three years later, the company opened an Accident and Liability Department, which handled employers' liability and workmen's collective insurance. Throughout its history, Aetna has made strategic investments to focus on health care and in 2017 CVS Health acquired the company for $69 billion.[22]

Aetna's tagline, "We're a health care company that's building a healthier world," is an admirable goal and a tall task. With 39 million members Aetna offers an array of plans and services, medical, pharmacy and dental plans, Medicare plans, Medicaid services, behavioral health programs, and medical management. Plans are based on the number of employees: 2–100, 101–4,999 and 5,000+. Aetna offers PPO, HMO, and Indemnity plans as well what it calls Exclusive Provider Organization (EPO), which gives "employees an easy way to get care, while saving on benefits costs with an exclusive network."[23] Aetna offers four EPO plans, one of which may be a good fit for your company, especially the self-funded Open Access Select Plan[SM].

The next section will review individual, family, and group policies. For employers, the group policies are the most relevant if they offer health insurance for their employees.

Medical Insurance Policies

Individual and Family Policies

The self-employed, early retirees, and employees whose companies did not sponsor health insurance typically purchased individual and family policies prior to 2014. With the passage of the Affordable Care Act (ACA), popularly known as Obamacare, individual health and family insurance policies have undergone a major transformation since the ACA became operational in 2014. When individuals/families didn't have employer-sponsored coverage or government-run health care coverage prior to the passage of Obamacare, the insurance they purchased tended to be less expensive than most group coverage for a simple reason. These policies were medically underwritten, which meant that individuals with preexisting conditions either could not get coverage or the cost was prohibitively expensive. Insurers gladly wrote policies for general healthy subscribers who did not have much medical costs during any given year. In addition, the individual plans typically offered less coverage than a group plan.[24]

The ACA markedly reduced the differences in coverage between individual and employer-sponsored plans. Under the ACA, individual plans mandated 10 "essential health benefits," with no annual lifetime dollar cap. Previously, "only 2 percent of individual major medical health insurance plans were providing coverage for all ten of the essential health benefits that are now standard on all plans purchased since January 1, 2014." In addition, these policies could not exclude individuals with preexisting conditions.[25]

The ACA plans have four "metal" designations—Bronze, covering 60 percent of costs; Silver, 70 percent; Gold, 80 percent; and Platinum 90 percent. Platinum plans have limited availability for individuals generally available in the small group market. These plans can be purchased at HealthCare.gov for most Americans who need an ACA-compliant individual policy; 14 states and the DC have created their own state platforms. The federal government provides tax credits for individual plans and a cost-sharing subsidy based on household income but only if a plan is purchased through a government exchange. (In 2020, 86 percent of the 11.3 million who bought policies on the exchanges were eligible for subsidies.) Furthermore, individuals and families have a maximum $8,550 and $17,100 annual out-of-pocket expense (in 2021), respectively.[26]

Note that in some states only one insurer is available, others have many insurers on the exchanges, and premiums do vary based on age, zip code, tobacco use, and which insurance company you choose. Gender or medical history does not affect the insurance premium as they did prior to the passage of the ACA.[27] Thus, shopping for a plan on the national exchange or your state website is a worthwhile undertaking because the savings could be substantial. (See www.talktomira.com/post/how-much-does-obama-care-cost, for an overview of Obamacare plan costs by tiers.)

Group Policies

Although an employer-based group policy is available for businesses of all sizes, the focus in this section will be on small businesses with less than 50 employees. Businesses with 50 employees or more are subject the ACA mandate, which requires employers to provide health insurance. Nevertheless, the cost of small group policies can vary markedly by costs and there are numerous plans to choose from. Such policies may require at least 70 participation rate; employees join voluntarily; premiums are typically shared between the employer and employees; an employee can pay to add family members. (There is no free lunch here.)[28]

A group plan is usually less expensive than individual plans because the risk pool is greater, a major feature of insurance, which spreads the risk among a number of individuals. In addition, an employer's monthly premiums are generally tax-deductible and a small business may be eligible for a health care tax credit; employees too get a tax break, because they pay their premiums with pre-tax dollars, reducing their taxable income.[29]

Group health plans do not have a specific enrollment period during the year and can be purchased through professional organizations and associations. Typical group plans include HMOs and PPOs, which were discussed previously in the chapter.[30]

Small business owners can make an informed decision about the myriad types of plans by visiting the ehealthinsurance.org page, www .ehealthinsurance.com/resources/small-business/the-complete-guide-to-selecting-the-best-small-business-health-insurance-plan. This overview can help small businesses navigate the insurance maze that has been unfolding for decades. There are fledgling alternatives to traditional insurance plans/arrangements that may be more cost-effective and provide better coverage for employees of not only small businesses but also businesses of any size. The remaining chapters will review these alternatives so that businesses will have even more choices to consider in a health sector dominated by several large insurance companies.

CHAPTER 5

Evolution in Employer-Based Medical Care

For decades, employers provided traditional group insurance policies for their employees. These policies were reviewed in Chapter 4, highlighting the strengths and weaknesses of these policies. In this chapter, we will review how employer-based insurance has evolved in order to reduce costs and give employees some options, which they did not have under a group plan.

Employers have had essentially two group plan options for their employees: a fully insured plan or self-insured health plan. In a fully insured plan, an employer pays a premium to an insurance company, which in turn covers employees' medical expenses. Employees typically have a co-pay for an office visit, a medical procedure, or hospital stay, and pay a deductible before the insurance company makes any payment to the medical provider. Insurance premiums are tax-deductible for the employer and provide tax-free benefits for employees. Companies thus do not have to deal with claims and other administrative tasks, which are typically handled by the insurance company.

Historically, especially in the first few decades of the 20th century, manufacturing companies hired a physician to be on the premises to deal with employees' illnesses or accidents. The doctors thus were company employees. Over the years, more and more companies have used this self-insured method; in other words, self-funded employee medical expenses. Eventually, this approach became attractive to employers because it allows them to customize the medical needs of their employees and usually lowers the costs of insurance. However, the risk of insurance falls on the company instead of the insurance company in a traditional insurance policy. To handle expensive or catastrophic claims, an employer typically purchases stop-loss or excess-loss insurance that pays for claims above a certain amount of outlays. Moreover, an employer will incur fees to pay for on-site staff, third-party administrators, and software fees to handle their employees' claims.

Health Reimbursement Arrangements

In recent years, employers created health reimbursement arrangements (HRAs), which have several plans for employers to choose from. Needless to say, these arrangements became subject to government regulations (1974 ERISA and 1996 HIPPA rules) that required benefits to be equalized among employees. In other words, employers could not offer more benefits to an employee who was in the same class as similar employees.[1]

In June 2002, the Internal Revenue Service (IRS) and again in 2013 issued regulations that limited companies' use of HRAs. However, in 2016 the Small Business Healthcare Relief Act made HRAs less restrictive for employers and thus made them more attractive for employers with less than 50 employees to offer an alternative to traditional group insurance. In doing so, it created a new HRA, the Qualified Small Employer Health Reimbursement Arrangement (QSEHRA).[2] Two years later, several cabinet departments, at behest of President Trump, issued proposed regulations, which were finalized in June 2019. A new HRA was born, the individual coverage HRA (ICHRA).

The ICHRA is available to any size business and has greater flexibility because there are no allowance caps and employers can "very eligibility and allowance amounts among different classes of employees."[3]

Employers now have another option using a HRA called group coverage HRA (GCHRA). Under this arrangement, employees pay for medical expenses out of their HRA allowance, which aren't covered by the employees' group plan, and with a high deductible plan, premium costs are lowered.

Which HRA is best for both employers and employees? The answer, of course, depends on how employers want to provide coverage for their employees to keep costs in check and give employees an affordable way to pay for their medical expenses.

Let's start with an overview of a qualified small employer HRA (QSEHRA). Only employers with less than 50 full-time employees can create one. An employer who has 51 employees or slightly more cannot offer this coverage, even though it may be beneficial to his or her employees who want to have more control over their medical coverage. Employers cannot offer a group health insurance policy and provide a QSEHRA. It is one or the other. The essence of this plan is that employees receive a tax-free reimbursement for their health insurance payments and other out-of-pocket expenses. Employees cannot take their accounts with them; they stay with the employer. Employees have to be covered by a minimum essential coverage policy (MEC). An MEC is an insurance policy that meets the standards of the Affordable Care Act, popularly known as Obamacare. These policies must cover a minimum 60 percent of costs and provide 10 essential health benefits.[4]

Should your small business provide a qualified small employer HRA? For employers who do not want the hassle of navigating which group plan is best for their company and willing to set aside a monthly allowance for their employees to pay for them medical coverage, this makes perfect sense. There are limits to how much employer can contribute to a QSEHRA. For 2022 employers can contribute $454.16 per month and $5,450 per year for a single employee. The maximum contribution for an employee with the family is $11,050 per year or $920.83 per month. These funds can be used to pay for more than 200 eligible expenses as well as health insurance premiums, co-pays, deductibles, prescription, and over-the-counter drugs as well as chiropractic visits.[5]

All qualified expenses must be approved by a company administrator or third party. One of the attractive features of a QSEHRA is that the monthly allowance can be rolled over into the next month. Employees cannot get reimbursed for the amount that is in the account for that month. In other words, employees have to shop around to get the best possible "deals" for their medical expenses and thus become "savvy" medical consumers. One potential glitch in this HRA for employees is if they do not have an insurance policy or one that does not meet the MEC guidelines the reimbursements are taxable.[6]

An individual coverage HRA (ICHRA) is available to all employers, including nonprofits, and can be offered to employees who also could be covered by an employer group health plan. This benefit is based on reimbursements that are not subject to payroll or income taxes. Employers

have discretion in creating "classes" of employees whose benefits are determined by the company and setting allowance caps for employees. There
is no maximum contribution limit. Employees, in turn, decide on the
coverage they want to purchase and out-of-pocket expenses they will pay.[7]

To participate in an ICHRA, an employee must have an individual
health insurance policy and inform the HRA administrator in order to
receive reimbursements. After the administrator reviews the detailed submitted expense, the employee is reimbursed.[8]

A group coverage HRA (GCHRA) allows employers who offer group
health insurance and want to provide a monthly allowance for employees
to pay for deductibles, co-pays, and out-of-pocket expenses. The IRS lists
the more than 200 eligible expenses that can be covered by a GCHRA.
The flexibility of a GCHRA helps employers who are able to offer a generous health insurance benefits package attract more employees than
companies that have "tighter" employee expense budgets.

A side-by-side comparison of all three HRAs can be found at www
.peoplekeep.com/health-reimbursement-arrangement-hra. This snapshot
should be one of the first steps employers could take to begin a review of
their employee health benefits. From there, employers could then speak
with a health benefits consultant or insurance agent to craft a plan that
meets their and employees' needs.

Health Savings Accounts

Medical savings accounts, a precursor to HSAs, were introduced as an
amendment to HIPPA in 1996. Although a limited number (750,000
taxpayers) of MSAs were allowed initially, only 150,000 were created
because of the complexity of the rules. Health Savings Accounts was eventually passed in the Congress in 2003 as part of an overhaul of Medicare,
which included adding a prescription benefit (Medicare Prescription,
Improvement and Modernization Act (MMA)). Although the bill contained five restrictions on HSAs, the huge benefit for employees are manifold. Employees fund their HSAs with pre-tax dollars; funds grow tax-free
and can be withdrawn tax-free. A triple tax-free bonanza![9]

Employers can contribute to an employee's HSA. Funds can roll
over year after year. Only qualified medical expenses can be paid by an

HSA; otherwise, the funds are subject to an income tax and a 20 percent penalty. Employees must purchase a high deductible insurance policy to qualify for an HSA, and the account is portable.[10] Employees own the account and thus changing employers becomes an easier decision to make, as health benefits can be a "deal breaker" for anyone looking to move on or relocate.

In 2022, an individual can contribute up to $3,650 while a family can contribute up to $7,300. Contributions can be made monthly or via payroll withholding and be adjusted anytime. Employees who are 55 years old or older can "catch up" and deposit an additional $1,000 annually. In addition, adult children who live with their parents are covered as long as they are younger than 26 years. Another interesting use of an HSA is employees could pay out of pocket for minor medical expenses, which would allow all these funds to grow. And when a major expense in the future occurs, the HSA could be used to pay for a down payment on a house, college tuition, and so on, up to the amount that was paid for qualified medical expenses in the past.[11]

The good news for employees is that employers can offer both an HRA and HSA. A "limited purpose HRA" can only cover expenses not covered by an HSA deductible requirement such as health insurance premium, long-term care premium, wellness/preventive care, such as checkups, mammograms, smoking cessation, weight loss, dental expenses, and vision expenses.[12]

SHRM®, the Society of Human Resource Management, posted an article by Stephen Miller, "Health Care Consumerism: HSAs and HRAs," (www.shrm.org/resourcesandtools/hr-topics/benefits/pages/hrasandhsasanoverview.aspx), which provides a comprehensive overview of the two popular consumer-driven health plans. Employers can review the side-by-side comparisons and have a conversation with their employees about the benefits of each arrangement.

Miller cites a consultancy report that asserts for employers whose workforce is comprised primarily of young, healthy individuals, an HRA makes a lot of sense. The HRA could be used for emergency room visits and hospital stays. The individuals would pay out of pocket for routine office visits. If an employer has more middle-aged and senior workers, prescription drug coverage in addition to office visits hospital stays, and outpatient surgeries would be considered an advisable HRA package.

For HR managers, a conversation about an HRA or HSA is essential, if they are considering moving away from a traditional group insurance benefit. The last thing a company would like to see is employee morale decline if the health benefits are not aligned with the "culture" of the workforce. In other words, a health benefits package must be a win–win for both employers and employees. The flexibility of HRAs and HSAs can be a huge selling point for employers to attract individuals to their companies. Educating employees about the options regarding their health benefits requires having all the data and strengths and weaknesses of each approach readily available.

Cigna's "Maximizing The Value of Consumer-Driven Health Plans" analyzes the company's experience with both plans (www.cigna.com/static/www-cigna-com/docs/employers-brokers/882377-cdhp-white-paper-final.pdf). A major takeaway is that CDHPs "have been generally been found to be more effective than traditional plans in terms of reducing total medical costs, especially in the short run." Although I will discuss the future of health care in Chapter 10, Cigna believes that the genie is out of the bottle; CDHP are the wave of the future coupled with a pay-for-performance medical care model. Instead of a traditional fee for service to pay for medical care, the evolution to more accountability has become the latest alternative to the traditional health insurance model, with the goal of lowering costs and improving quality. In short, changes have been underway in the way employers provide health care benefits. Finding the suitable health benefits package can be daunting, but navigating the medical insurance maze does not have to be intimidating as long as small business owners and corporate executives obtain objective information.

Flexible Savings Accounts

Flexible savings accounts (FSA) were created in 1970s, which allows employees to use pretext dollars for qualified medical expenses that employers' medical plans did not cover. All eligible employees have a choice of three FSAs: a Health Care FSA, a Limited Purpose FSA, and a Dependent FSA. Health Care FSA covers employee expenses; a Limited Purpose FSA (which must be coupled with an HSA) covers eligible dental and vision expenses; and a Dependent FSA covers eligible dependents and disabled dependents.[13]

For 2022, employees can direct their companies to deduct as much as $2,850 from their paycheck to fund their Health FSAs. In addition, employers can contribute to their employees' FSA, and those funds do not count toward the employee's maximum contribution. The annual amount is indexed for inflation. And employees can carry over as much as $570 of FSA funds into the next year.

A dependent care FSA can pay for "day care, preschool, summer camps and non-employer sponsored before or after school programs." The Dependent Care maximum deferral for 2022 is $5,000 for single taxpayers and married couples filing jointly. An employer can contribute to this FSA, but any amount is applied to the individual annual maximum. In addition, employees may tap their FSA to pay for commuting costs. And a generous excludable amount of $14,890 can be used for adoption expenses. This amount is phased out, beginning with an income of $223,410 and is complete at $263,410.[14]

In sum, which is best for your company, HRA, HSA, or FSA, or some combination of these plans? Although there is no one-size-fits-all combination, Gabrielle Smith has put all three plans side-by-side to give employers a quick overview of how to begin unpacking the benefits and potential costs of consumer-driven health plans (www.peoplekeep.com/blog/hra-vs-hsa-vs-fsa-comparison-chart).

Health Maintenance Accounts

An innovative method for employers to help employees pay for some of their medical expenses is to offer them a HMA.® A HMA® is similar to an HSA but with a slight twist. Employees make monthly contributions into an account that grows over 36 months, and at the end of the period the funds have increased by approximately $2 for every dollar deposited. This is illustrated in www.healthmatchingaccounts.com/hma-account-balance-growth-explanation/. According to the explanation page, "The HMA® creates more health care purchasing power and freedom than ever before and leads to additional health care savings for individuals and families by covering a larger portion of their out-of-pocket, medical expenses than any other medical savings account available."[15] The FAQ page provides the basic information to assist employers determine if the HMA® would be an integral medical care benefits package to retain and/or attract employees.[16]

All businesses have to compete for the public's dollars and have to provide value for customers; otherwise a competitor will gobble up that revenue stream. One way to keep costs in check is to streamline health care benefits while providing value to employees, which should help attract competent individuals to grow the company. For business decision makers, a strategic initiative should be to "partner" with their employees to hold down health care benefits costs. Although this is easier said than done, the innovations and more friendly regulatory environment give employers more options than ever, which I will explore in the next several chapters.

CHAPTER 6

Direct Primary Care

The old adage, "necessity is the mother of invention," is nowhere more applicable than the experience of Garrison Bliss, MD who describes himself as a "proud Direct Primary Care pioneer," and served as president of the American Academy of Private Physicians. Dr. Bliss's journey to embrace Direct Primary Care as a way to bring compassionate care to his patients began when his son was presumed to have a digestive disorder, causing him to endure a month-long episode of vomiting. Dr. Bliss's son, Michael, was examined by a pediatrician with knowledge of oncology who diagnosed him a with a cerebellar ependymoma (a tumor from the ependymal cells, which line the ventricles of the brain and the central canal of the spinal cord). After it was removed, Michael wanted bacon to satisfy his hunger. Michael's nurse informed Dr. Bliss that she could not order the bacon "until the doctors finished their rounds." At the time Dr. Bliss realized his son's immediate needs were overridden or ignored by the nurses and doctors in the hospital.[1]

Soon after this episode, Dr. Bliss began to reevaluate health care in general and his medical practice specifically. He concluded that he needed to focus more on his patients and developed a four-pronged approach. His practice's new structure included: (1) more time with patients, (2) more room for urgent care, (3) clearer promises, and (4) better patient experiences. In short, the foundation for the Direct Primary Care movement began. Dr. Bliss realized that a relatively low monthly fee—at the time (1990s) estimated between $30 and $50 per patient per month and a patient panel between 600 and 800—would achieve his goal of a new medical practice. His Seattle-based practice opened in 1997 and he filled his patient load in slightly more than 12 months.[2]

In 2001, Dr. Brian R. Forrest was the first family physician in the country to open a Direct Primary Care (DPC) practice in Apex, North Carolina, Access Healthcare (www.acchealth.com). Dr. Forrest's inspiration for a DPC practice came from a gym membership. A gym membership includes access to all the equipment instead of having to pay a fee to use dumbbells, a treadmill, etc. Using the equipment in an all-inclusive fee thus makes patrons healthier. He explains that a DPC practice allows him to devote 100 percent of his time meeting patients face-to-face, and he does not "have to do any of the baloney with insurance."[3]

Becoming a DPC doctor had a major challenge, namely, facing financial insecurity while building a practice over a year or more. But once the transition is made, according to Dr. Forrest, "the pay is actually better than traditional medicine."[4]

For Dr. Jeffrey S. Gold, watching his mother care for his grandmother who had dementia was a difficult experience, especially since the family physician had very little involvement. After he became a physician and worked in a major hospital system for nine years, he was disillusioned with "big health care" early on. When he learned about DPC, he decided to open his practice (2015), Gold Direct Care (golddirectcare.com) in Marblehead, Massachusetts. He points out DPC is "real" medicine by not having to deal with paperwork, bureaucracy, and insurance. Dr. Gold believes the American people are "brainwashed" about health care, thinking it is so expensive that they need insurance to pay their medical care bills. And a major reason health care is expensive is because of "having a third party pay for it," Dr. Gold points out.[5]

Dr. Nate Favini, founder of Forward, a direct primary care service with locations in California, New York City, and Long Island as well as in several other large cities, wanted to be doctor since he was five years old, when his father, an emergency physician, bemoaned the fact that patients in the emergency room (ER) did not have accessible primary care and died prematurely from cancer, heart disease, and other treatable diseases. Young Nate decided he wanted to be a primary care doctor; he began his medical care career at a Bronx, New York, community health center, where patients were packed in the waiting room like sardines and had to wait for hours to see a doctor who typically spent 10 minutes with a patient.[6] After learning about the history of health care in America, Dr. Favini decided to build from the ground up a primary care practice, Forward (www.goforward.com) that would use high tech to provide preventative care.

The philosophy at Forward can be summed up in its mission: "to radically improve how healthcare works in order to *lower costs,* improve results and make quality care available to those who need it most"[7] (emphasis added). Launched in San Francisco (2017), Forward began to use genetic testing to screen for cancer and heart disease, and the following year introduced a body scanner to assist doctors in identifying potential diseases. Innovations since then include an app to monitor a patient's mental health for anxiety and depression and a Dermatascope to detect skin cancer. In short, Forward uses high tech to diagnose and treat a major illness before it becomes an expensive treatment in a hospital.[8]

Forward is committed to strengthening the doctor–patient relationship by having blood and other tests done in-house so the results can be analyzed by the physician and discussed with the patient instead of the patient having to make another appointment. Forward's goal, therefore, is to keep patients healthy rather than treating sickness, calling the current system "sick care," because the doctor only sees you when patients are ill. At Forward, their approach is just the opposite, and working with individuals to achieve optimal health before a major illness or disease strikes. Thus, at Forward, patients are welcome, encouraged to see their physicians often and utilize the services to monitor risks based on a patient's "unique biology."[9]

Direct Primary Care (DPC) turns primary medical care on its head by providing virtually 24/7 access to a physician; having no co-pays or deductibles without an insurance company gatekeeper; and patients get more time with a physician, eliminating seemingly endless waiting time in a doctor's office and other benefits. As of 2018, there were about 20,000 DPC physicians out of approximately 465,000 physicians nationwide, or 4.5 percent.[10] In short, there is substantial growth potential in the number of DPC doctors who could transform primary care into a more "entrepreneurial" model rather than the traditional fee-for-service primary care doctor's office, where each physician may have as many 2,500 patients.

For patients, the benefits of having a physician "on call" 24/7 is appealing. Not having to wait days for an appointment is another plus in participating in a DPC practice. Getting routine tests in the doctor's office and the results immediately is also a major benefit, which reduces the anxiety of waiting to learn about a possible illness and receiving treatment ASAP.

For physicians who have a DPC practice, the overwhelming consensus is the feeling they are practicing medicine the way they thought it would be to benefit their patients. Instead of worrying about entering the correct code for an insurance claim and having to hire administrative staff to handle the billing, the reduction in overhead costs makes a DPC practice more efficient than a fee-for-service practice. In short, the "burnout" factor for DPC doctors is virtually nil—a very good thing for patients who want their physicians in the best frame of mind to diagnose and treat their illnesses competently.

Employers and Direct Primary Care

This section is based on a PowerPoint presentation ("The Perfect Health Benefit for Young Companies") by FreedomDocs.com, a website dedicated to promoting Direct Primary Care for employers, individuals, and physicians. Christopher Habig, CEO and co-founder of FreedomHealthworks.com, created the content and has allowed me to share with you how health care must be based on doctor–patient relationship, "free of barriers," so patients can obtain value in the health care marketplace.

A major—if not the primary—consideration for individuals in deciding which company to work for is the health benefits package. A health benefits package could be a "deal breaker" for a prospective employee if he or she is not convinced there would be adequate medical care coverage for himself and his family. FreedomDocs provides a solution for startups and mature companies. For example, health benefits must be structured to not only attract talent but retain them as well. Entrepreneurs should devote their efforts on the company's mission to provide customers with a product or service that has value to them and not spend time on collecting employee data and then send that information to insurance brokers for a quote to determine which carrier is preferable. Instead, a DPC benefit would allow employers to plan better because at a fixed, predictable cost per head (x dollars per month); thus, an entrepreneur would be able to budget new hires much more easily than providing traditional medical care insurance, where the costs could be inflated depending on the number of dependents and other variables. In addition, DPC eliminates the broker, middlemen, undoubtedly a potentially substantial savings.

An employee health benefit has several components.

- Primary care
- Ancillary: imaging (MRI), lab testing, and prescriptions
- Specialist care—surgical procedures, physical therapy, and consultations
- Catastrophic care—hospital and emergency
- Vision
- Dental

Thus, beginning with primary care, "the perfect health benefit," employees would have access to "concierge-level" type customer service, which is valued by patients because it is utilized most often. DPC includes acute and urgent care, chronic condition management, preliminary mental health services, and discounted ancillary services, especially in-office dispensed prescriptions. Examples of usage would include a routine office visit, urgent care, telehealth, navigating downstream care, and pharmaceuticals.

The next "perfect health benefit," specialty care, would consist of a FreedomDoc^{SM} affiliate network where employees would get discounted consultations to avoid unnecessary testing and procedures, discounted cash payment procedures, such as surgeries, physical therapy, and other medical care. Also included would be an annual eye exam and dental care membership, which would provide two exams, two cleaning, one set of X-rays, and 20 percent discount on elective services. Accordingly, for example, an insurance-based hospital knee replacement would cost just under $45,000, but at an independent surgery center, the cost would be $15,500. Thus, insurance premiums would reflect the costs of a hospital-provided benefits, which is why the insurance premium for a family of four is now more than $21,000 annually. And if a family is generally healthy, a traditional insurance policy is a very expensive way to obtain medical care.

The next "perfect health benefit" is catastrophic care, based on a health share membership. An employee would receive "self-pay" discounts for all non-primary care. For example, an insurance-based childbirth could cost $42,000 with a maximum out-of-pocket expense of $11,000. A cash-priced OB and delivery would be $7,300 and only a $1,000 out-of-pocket expense.

What would a sample benefits package cost the employer, assuming the company would pay for all the benefits? A total of $380 per month is broken down as follows.

• FreedomDoc^{SM} PCP (primary care physician)	$90 per month
• Catastrophic health share	$250 per month
• Dental	$20 per month
• Vision	$20 per month
• Discounted affiliate specialist network	included
• Discounted ancillary services	included

Reproduced with permission of Freedomdocs.

A flat-rate pricing would allow an employer to easily determine the cost of hiring a new employee and possibly lure talent from competitors with an innovative way to provide health care, which would mean a higher salary, allowing the employee to pay out of pocket for medical care expenses at deeply discounted prices.

For example, an employee, let's call him Phil, would choose a DPC physician of his choice and there would be no co-pays or deductibles or additional cost from an executive physical exam to any treatment that could be handled in an office visit. Urgent care visits would be in the office rather than a hospital ER or an urgent care clinic. Phil would also have the ability to call, text, or have a video chat with his doctor 24/7. Other services that Phil could access include diet/nutrition, exercise guidance, and questions about new therapies. In addition, Phil would get basic dental and optometrist checkups as needed and discounts for non-covered procedures.

What would Phil's out-of-pocket expenses be? Discounted prescriptions in his doctor's office and recommendations for discounts at other providers. If Phil needed an magnetic resonance imaging (MRI) scan, a local hospital may charge as much as $4,000 paid by insurance (which drives up the cost of traditional insurance premiums), but an out-of-pocket cost for him may be $400 at an affiliated imaging center. And if Phil needs a lipid panel test, which could cost as much as $300, his doctor's deep discount affiliated lab may charge only $25.

If Phil needs more costly care, what are his options? His doctor may recommend a podiatrist, for example, if a specialist is needed to assess his condition. Phil could then get a consultation for an independent podiatrist, not just a local provider but also one in another part of the country for a telemedicine session. Prices for all the available doctors would be known beforehand so Phil could make a choice and determine which doctor provides the better value.

Most surgeries are elective, which would allow Phil to do research to obtain the best value for his medical care dollars. And finally, a catastrophic insurance policy would protect Phil and his family from a major illness and thus allay any anxiety about exorbitant medical bills.

At https://freedomdoc.care/business/, businesses "of all shapes and sizes can have a FreedomDoc experience" by first obtaining the information they need to make an educated decision about the health care they want to provide employees. Employees too can learn about the FreedomDoc approach (https://freedomdoc.care/memberships/), which puts them and their doctors at the center of medical care decisions instead of expensive traditional employer-based medical insurance.

Criticism of Direct Primary Care

According to Direct Primary Care's proponents, individuals and families get quality, relatively low-cost health care. Nevertheless, is there any downside to having employees enrolled in a DPC plan? Yes, asserts management professor Timothy Hoff, who focuses on health care systems and health policy at Northeastern University. Hoff does not believe DPC is a "transformative innovation for making primary care more relevant, responsive, and affordable on a large scale."[11]

Thus, Huff points out that "direct primary care is self-limiting in how many patients it can serve." True. That's what makes DPC attractive to both doctors and patients, practicing medicine the way it is supposed to be, namely, not bound by a 15-minute office visit and having access to your doctor virtually 24/7. Hoff rightly acknowledges that the country is facing a primary doctor access problem and DPC would exacerbate it. He also asserts "too many sicker or needier patients can also be problematic for direct primary doctors, as they require more contact and management."

However, the goal of DPC, according to Dr. Favini, founder of Forward, is to help patients get and stay healthy, not just having doctors treat them for illnesses. If optimal health is the goal of every individual, then a DPC practice would be a worthwhile health care option for individuals who have chronic illnesses that can be successfully treated by a primary care physician.

Professor Hoff also asserts that the DPC model has an incentive to limit care. He points out DPC doctors obtain their revenue via a monthly retainer and thus take on the financial risk for lab work and screenings. Thus, Hoff concludes, this "imposes significant pressure to keep service utilization, care management activity, and direct contact per patient lower to maximize the profit margin." He does not offer any data to support his assertion.

Another criticism leveled by Hoff is that patients could pay more for health care if they enroll in a DPC. The cost of the monthly retainer plus additional insurance, which would require co-pays and deductibles, could exceed the cost of having traditional insurance coverage.

Lastly, Hoff makes an interesting criticism of DPC, namely, patients have to take on greater responsibility for their health care. This is not entirely accurate. No matter what type of health insurance individuals have, they have to read the fine print of their policy the employer has chosen for them or read through different policies if they have to choose from one.

In his conclusion, Hoff attempts to minimize the benefits of DPC, because he claims physicians in this practice downplay the role of hospitals and specialists, which are integral components of the health care system. From the DPC literature I have reviewed, this is far from the truth. DPC doctors and websites like FreedomDocs focus on the benefits of a small panel of patients that direct primary doctors serve and the ability to get specialists' services at deep discounts. Thus, DPC may, in fact, not be a panacea for every company, but it is an option to pursue that could be in the best interests for both employees and employers.

Conclusion

The DPC model is gaining speed across the country. WebMD published, "More Patients Turning to 'Direct Primary Care,'"[12] highlighting how DPC employers have determined this benefit makes sense for their employees. For example, Mick Lowedermann, father of two small children and owner of the 12-employee pest control business in Wichita, Kansas, contracted with Atlas MD for a cost of $50 monthly fee per employee and customized major medical insurance policy for which he pays $375 monthly per employee. According to Lowerdermann, traditional insurance policy would be double or triple that cost.

The bottom line from employers is that a well-structured DPC benefit package in conjunction with a major medical/catastrophic insurance policy could eliminate having to navigate the medical insurance maze that is expensive and bureaucratic.

CHAPTER 7

Concierge Medicine

Just for the Wealthy?

If a poll were conducted about the most frustrating things in life, waiting in a doctor's office would undoubtedly be near the top, if not at the top of the list. On average, the wait time to see your doctor is about 18 minutes and possibly greater if a patient before you needs more than the 15- to 20-minute average visit at a traditional practice, which could have as many as 5,000 patients under one doctor's care.[1] In other words, a traditional medical practice could best be described as "assembly line" medical care, where a physician may see anywhere between 30 and 50 patients per day. No wonder physician burnout is a real phenomenon while patients are rightly concerned that their care is almost an afterthought.

A traditional medical practice, therefore, is not an optimal process to diagnose and treat every patient empathically given the little time a physician spends in the examining room. Undoubtedly, there are physicians in traditional practices that are excellent diagnosticians who treat their patients with respect and compassion. Nevertheless, the short time a patient has with a physician could mean an incorrect diagnosis and inappropriate treatment. This could be catastrophic for the patient. Employers thus have an obligation to their employees who receive their medical care benefits as part of their compensation package to provide them, given the financial constraints of every business, the least frustrating, highest quality medical coverage possible for obvious reasons.

An appealing patient-centered health care benefits package would tend to reduce absenteeism, increase morale, increase productivity, attract new talent, and, maybe most important, retain key employees who have helped make your business a success.[2] In the last chapter we saw how

Direct Primary Care (DPC), according to its advocates, fulfills the mission of creating an optimal doctor–patient relationship by charging a relatively a low-cost monthly fee to have a same day or a next day visit rather than the typical traditional medical practice where an appointment may not be available for days or sometimes a week or more in advance. Is there another alternative to DPC that employers could offer their employees to eliminate what seems like interminable delays in a physicians' waiting room? Enter concierge medicine (CM), which is similar to DPC and is usually thought of as medical care for the "rich and famous." Not anymore.

Brief History of Concierge Medicine

The genesis of concierge medicine began in 1996 when two doctors created MD2 (pronounced MD squared) in the Pacific Northwest. They charged an annual fee of $13,000 and $20,000 per family. In other words, this pricey new health care structure was out of the reach for most families except high-income individuals who wanted in effect to escape a traditional medical practice. These upper-income families wanted to get a more personalized health care experience.[3]

Insofar medical care is highly regulated at all levels of government, concierge medicine, although only a relatively small segment of healthcare, has grown markedly in the 25 years it was first offered to the public as an alternative to a traditional medical practice. Bioethicists as well as the American Medical Association (AMA) have weighed in on the ethics of concierge medicine with guidelines, given the perception of CM as an "elitist" practice that should not violate fundamental ethical principles that physicians should abide by to treat all their patients compassionately.

The Pros and Cons of Concierge Medicine

So what is concierge medicine? And could CM replace traditional medical insurance for employees? For employers, would having CM as a component of their benefits package set them apart from competitors as a more desirable business to work for?

A concierge medicine physician charges an annual fee or retainer, which could be paid quarterly or monthly depending on the practice's billing options. The annual costs can vary from $1,500 to as much as $20,000 depending on the array of services offered.[4] The former amount is atypical of most CM practices, which have gone "mainstream" to attract a greater pool of patients.

For the annual fee, a patient receives 24/7 access to a physician who usually has no more than a 500–600-patient panel. The CM doctor is virtually indistinguishable from a traditional primary care physician who conducts annual physicals, orders lab tests, provides diagnostic tests, treats both cuts with stitches, and minor skin conditions. Specialized treatments are referred to other doctors as well as surgeries that have to be performed in an outpatient center or hospital.

Concierge doctors have the same education and medical training—around 11 years after graduating from high school—to obtain a license to practice medicine.

A CM patient can expect shorter wait time to see a doctor in the office during normal business hours. And if a nonthreatening emergency occurs during the wee hours overnight, one doctor is typically available to treat the patient.

For example, one New York City CM patient with Parkinson's disease fell backward at 3 a.m. in the bathroom and hit her head. Her husband who previously took his wife to the emergency room for medical treatment had to spend five hours to see a doctor and be discharged. This time the couple in their seventies who had contracted with a nearby CM practice called the office and were told to come in immediately where they were met by the medical team that performed a CT scan. The CT scan was negative. Only 40 minutes went by from the time of the call to the reading of the results. This couple had paid $10,000 annually for this CM service in Manhattan.[5] A Manhattan CM practice is indeed expensive and out of the reach of most families.

Since this story was published in 2018, the CM practice in the article changed its name to Sollis Health (see https://sollishealth.com). Employers can access the page devoted to them and see if this medical care benefit would make a good fit for their employers. Sollis locations are limited to a few communities in California, New York, the Hamptons, and Florida. In other words, Sollis Health is to health care what high-end luxury cars are to the public. If you have to ask for the price, you probably cannot afford it. But the pricing structure is not out of reach for many upper middle-income families who would be willingly to pay up to $9,000 for a family of three, which would include a child under 18.

The founder of Sollis Health, Dr. Bernard Kruger, who is a board-certified physician in oncology and internal medicine, realized that a hospital emergency room leaves much to be desired for non-life-threatening care. Kruger brought a patient who fell off a horse to the emergency room at a local hospital and was met by the head of the department there. Nevertheless, Kruger's patient still had to wait five hours for a CAT scan. He realized there had to be a better alternative. He and his partners created Priority Private Care, now Sollis Health. In other words, there was—and still is—a problem in treating ER patients in a timely manner. Dr. Kruger's medical entrepreneurship took a problem and turned it into a thriving CM practice.[6]

We already remarked about the shorter wait time to see a CM doctor. Telemedicine visits can be handled almost immediately as well as phone and text messages. Office visits tend to be covered with the annual fee, but the CM practice may bill the patient's insurance company as an in or out of network provider. Unlimited visits for patients are particularly beneficial for anyone with chronic medical conditions such as diabetes, hypertension, or heart disease, to name a few.

One of the most attractive aspects of CM is the time a doctor spends with patients. This allows the doctor–patient relationship to grow so the physician has a much better grasp of the patient's overall health concerns and lifestyle to assist him or her with the necessary information, protocols, and treatments for optimal health.

For employees who have health savings accounts or flexible savings accounts, the cost of a CM membership may be paid out of these accounts. If these accounts can defray the out-of-pocket costs of the annual CM fee, then a concierge benefit may be even more attractive to employees, especially those whose income would allow them to purchase this service.

Despite the obvious benefits outlined above of having employees enrolled in a concierge medicine practice, there are drawbacks that both employers and employees should beware of when deciding if concierge medicine makes sense.

The cost of enrolling in a concierge medicine practice may not be considered a good value for employees if the only CM in their community is pricey and bills insurance companies for office visits. That means the employer would have to provide a traditional insurance policy for employees. If an employer does not pick up all or most of the cost of CM, then the employees may have an out-of-pocket expense they may not wish to incur and thus forgo all the benefits, which makes CM an attractive health care benefit.

On the other hand, if an employer could structure a health care benefits package that includes CM as the foundation and employer-paid insurance package that included hospitalization and emergency care, assuming such a package would meet the Affordable Care Act requirements, then the premium savings to the employer would be substantial.

A CM practice in an employer's community may not have physicians that employees necessarily want to have as their primary care doctors. This could be an insurmountable obstacle in offering a CM option to employees. Assuming employees have already chosen a primary care doctor, an employer could ask physicians in their community if they would consider moving from a traditional medical practice to becoming a CM practice. This may be too much of a burden for an employer to consider, in effect becoming a catalyst for doctors to restructure their medical practices. However, for some physicians, the possibility of having a CM practice may be "just what the doctor ordered"—in this case a company's HR manager—given the burnout of primary care physicians who have to see at least 40 patients per day to maintain a viable traditional medical practice.

The bottom line for employers is obvious. If a CM option is the only health care benefit a business would offer to employees, they would have to be willing to embrace concierge medicine as in their best interests—no waiting to see a doctor, 24/7 access to a doctor, virtual meetings available as well as immediate or almost immediate medical test results, and consultation with a doctor. This may be a lift too heavy for an HR manager to consider, namely changing the "culture" and expectation what a health care benefit should be. Nevertheless, employees in the COVID era may be amenable to having a CM practice as a health care option or the foundation of their health care benefits.

How would an employer approach employees regarding a CM practice health care benefits option? The short answer is with educating them after the HR manager performs the necessary due diligence with one of several CM consultants or any one of concierge medicine practices in your area.

American medical care is being transformed for a variety of reasons—the cost of traditional insurance premiums, accessibility to physicians in a timely manner, quality of care, and the insufferable amount of time spent waiting the see your doctor in the office. According to proponents of concierge medicine, CM addresses all these issues; therefore, it should be a win–win for employees, employers, and doctors. Concierge medicine has increased in popularity for the reasons patients give about the flaws in the current system. Whether it makes sense for your workforce can only be determined by providing employees with the pros and cons of CM for them to make an informed decision, assuming management has concluded that as a health care package.

CHAPTER 8

Cost-Sharing Arrangements

In Chapter 4, I explained how and why traditional employer-based health insurance is expensive. One of the major reasons that health insurance is so expensive is because insurance pays the costs of routine medical care, which must be paid from (excessive) premiums collected by insurance companies. If insurance companies collected premiums to pay for only extraordinary medical care costs, premiums would decline substantially, and health insurance would then adhere to sound principles of indemnification (paying for a loss according to the terms of the insurance policy). Instead, insurance companies must cover their expected payouts, which are then passed on to employers in the form of ever-rising premiums. Employers, in turn, reduce wages and salaries of employees to pay for the premiums. In recent years, however, employers have had employees pick up part of the insurance premiums directly.

Despite having been a fixture of employees' benefits package for decades, employers and employees, too, have expressed displeasure with this arrangement. For employees who want access to doctors outside of the insurance company's network can be frustrating, to say the least. Patients want freedom of choice, not barriers to getting the best medical care possible. Both employers and employees also decry the lack of transparency in medical costs. Consequently, more and more employers have been seeking health benefits alternatives for their employees.

Chapters 5, 6, and 7 reviewed alternatives to traditional employer-based health insurance and how employees can have more freedom of choice, employers can save valuable resources while providing employees with benefits that give them better quality health care and possibly higher wages and salaries.

The focus of this chapter is to discuss a non-insurance alternative called *cost sharing* that would pay for medical costs outlined in the arrangement the group sets down for its members. Because medical bills are not "guaranteed" to be paid by the group, cost sharing may seem too "risky" for both employers and employees. Yet, billions of dollars have been reimbursed to members in the past couple of decades. Moreover, cost sharing has a long history and tradition in America, going back to colonial times and blossomed throughout the 19th and early 20th centuries. In fact, one of the strengths of American culture has been the creation of voluntary associations to deal with medical care, unemployment, life insurance, and other social and economic issues.

In his sweeping examination about mutual aid societies, David T. Beito recounts how millions of "Americans received social welfare benefits from their fraternal societies."[1] These benefits were in effect a form of cost sharing, with life insurance playing a predominant role in providing a vital benefit to members of the fraternal societies. Accordingly, Beito points out, "Americans can also learn from studying the contrast between voluntary fraternal medical care and third-party payment systems such as private insurance and Medicaid."[2] However, as successful as the fraternal societies were in fulfilling their missions, Beito asserts it would be virtually impossible to replicate these institutions today. Nevertheless, he dismisses the idea that fraternal societies have no role to play in the country today, especially since they exalted such values as "thrift, mutualism and individual responsibility."[3] These values have been replaced, to some degree, with a culture of entitlement, lack of transparency and accountability, and a third payment system that increases moral hazard.

Fraternal organizations emphasized that to be a member, it was important to exhibit "moral behavior"—restrictions on alcohol and narcotics use and "proper" sexual conduct—to avoid illnesses and thus medical costs that could be avoided. In short, fraternal societies would refuse medical benefits for any member engaged in conduct it considered "inappropriate."[4] In other words, fraternal societies had two missions: to help members pay for necessary expenses and to make sure they had the values that would keep medical costs down and thus contributions needed to fund the societies would be affordable to low-income workers, many of whom were newly arrived immigrants.

One of the ways fraternal societies provided low-cost medical care to its members was to hire a "lodge doctor." According to Beito, members paid an annual fee as low as $1.20 per year to as much as $2.00.

Fees varied across the country, depending on local conditions. Although this arrangement smacks more of a direct primary care model, the point of highlighting the approach reveals how the necessity of providing medical care to a group whose membership was based on ethnicity, national origin, and trade category met the needs of primarily immigrant communities without relying on third party insurance.[5]

A major concern of some opinion leaders and others during the early 20th century was that compulsory medical insurance would substitute "paternalism for fraternalism." During the heated debates in the early 20th century, the proponents of fraternalism were able to carry the day and national compulsory health insurance was put on the backburner as the fraternal societies flourished. Nevertheless, the idea was planted in the minds of the public and influential physicians and others who embraced for similar or differing reasons the idea of medical care paternalism.[6]

The major takeaway from the history of America's fraternal societies regarding social services is that they provided low-cost benefits in keeping with the culture of the era, self-help, virtuous behavior, and voluntary community solutions. Nevertheless, the decline of the fraternal model of social services began with the financial challenges they faced during the Great Depression and continued throughout the postwar period as government programs, regulations, and other interventions co-opted the role of fraternal societies.[7]

Medical Sharing Arrangements

An up-to-date version of sharing arrangements that were widespread in America before the Great Depression is becoming more "mainstream" for both employers and employees who want a low-cost health care benefits alternative. Needless to say, low cost is not a panacea if high-quality medical care is not provided to patients who participate in a medical sharing network.

So what are the main features of a medical sharing arrangement (also called health-sharing ministries, health care-sharing programs, and health-sharing plans) that have captured the imagination of a portion of the business community and increasing members of the general public, even though the number of Americans who use this method to pay for medical bills is miniscule compared with traditional health care insurance provided by the major companies? (It is estimated that at least 1.5 million Americans participate in some form of health-sharing arrangement.)

A medical-sharing arrangement is quite simple. Members who meet the guidelines be they a religious-based criteria, personal behavior standards, etc.—set forth in the medical sharing company's (MSC) manual typically, pay a monthly fee depending on how many family members would participate in the plan. Fees vary depending (from $300–$500 per month) on the medical coverage the plan provides. These funds are then used to pay for qualified bills submitted by members after they pay out-of-pocket what is called an "initial uninsurable amount" by one MSC ranging from $500 to $5,000 or more. To be clear, there is no legally binding contract between members and the MSC to pay bills. That does not mean that members are in so-called no man's land regarding their medical bills. Quite the contrary; if members submit bills that are in line with the MSC's manual, medical bills would be paid.[8]

At Liberty HealthShare, a religious-based MSC founded in 1995, for example, the shareable medical expenses are comprehensive.

- Conventional or naturopathic physician visits
- Wellness and screening appointments
- Clinic visits
- Urgent care/emergency room visits
- Hospital care (inpatient or outpatient)
- Physical therapy
- Speech therapy
- Occupational therapy
- Respiratory therapy
- Home health care
- Medical testing
- X-rays
- Ambulance transport
- Vaccinations
- Prenatal and maternity care (program dependent)

Source: www.libertyhealthshare.org/what-is-shared

And some medical expenses are not shareable, such as preexisting conditions during the first year of membership, Tier 1–3 prescriptions, dental/vision expenses, expenses other than accidents, acute illness, or injury within the first 60 days of membership. To check the specific restrictions of each exclusion, a potential employer or individual member would need to check the company's website (https://libertyhealthshare .org/what-is-shared).

Other health care-sharing ministries include Christian Healthcare Ministries, Medi-Share Samaritan Ministries, United Refuah HealthShare, MCS Medical Cost Sharing, Altrua HealthShare, Freedom HealthShare, and Trinity HealthShare. The common components of virtually all health-share ministries are direct payment to providers from members' savings accounts; freedom to choose doctors and hospitals in a preferred provider organization (PPO), which allows the ministry to negotiate preferred prices for medical care; members can use non-PPO doctors or facilities but may not have most or any of their bills covered.[9]

The advantages of a health care–sharing ministry are manifold, according to Liberty Health Share.[10] Some of the benefits include monthly contributions determined by program options, no annual or lifetime limits, no termination after developing a medical condition, employment status does not affect membership, auditing by independent accounting firm to ensure financial stability, and members are encouraged to help other members to foster a "family" atmosphere.

The drawbacks are equally important for an employer to consider before selecting a sectarian-based health sharing arrangement.[11]

Many regulations consider health care–sharing insurance, so consumers have little or no legal protection if a claim is not paid, coverage is denied, or the ministry goes bankrupt.

Treasury letter 2016-0051 confirms that health care–sharing ministries don't qualify as minimum essential coverage (MEC) the ACA's employer mandate.

There are certain restrictions and payment caps relating to preexisting conditions. Certain preexisting conditions, such as diabetes, may require a member to pay an additional monthly amount along with standard membership fees.

Because health care–sharing ministries are faith-based organizations, they can have specific rules associated with membership. For example, members might be required to attend church regularly, abstain from tobacco and illegal drugs, and attest to a specific statement of faith.

A faith-based health-sharing arrangement may not work for some or many employers and their employees given the diversity of religious affiliations in America. Nevertheless, faith-based health-sharing ministries have a niche in cost sharing arrangement universe because it fills a major need—to reduce costs based on values and "proper behavior" of members that the ministries assert would lead to lower medical expenses and thus a win–win for both employees and employers.

Another health sharing plan, Sedera, founded by English physician Tony Dale, author of *The Cure for Healthcare: An Old World Doctor's Prescription for the New World Health System,* has a 45-page manual on its website explaining the basics of the nonprofit's approach to medical sharing (https:// assets.ctfassets.net/01zqqfy0bb2m/6sC6nAWP3BSPDOsdRXwi5h /7b0424fd1709e15a9422bdef2b6f0b94/Sedera_-_SELECT_Plus_ Guidelines_20210901.pdf). Not only does the manual provide generic information about medical sharing but also includes details how Sedera's guidelines would achieve the mission of the nonprofit, to provide low cost, transparent, high-quality medical care to employees and individual members. For employers who want to join a medical-sharing plan instead of the traditional third-party insurance, Sedera would be a good place to start to learn how this growing medical benefit would be a win–win for themselves and their employees.

Dr. Dale who journeyed from a London-based physician and witnessed the deficiencies of the British single-payer system to America, where he was a cash-paying patient, was appalled at the lack of transparency in medical care prices. He was determined to do something about it as a "medical entrepreneur." Dr. Dale tried to convince Christian health care ministries to include individuals and employers from all backgrounds, not adherents of one faith. His suggestion was rebuffed. Seeing an opportunity to make health sharing more mainstream, he founded Sedera in 2014. He recounts his story about the hurdles he faced to make his nonprofit company comply with federal and state regulations. Dr. Dale's book is a worthy addition to the growing literature on how to fix America's expensive health care system.

At MPB Health (https://mpb.health), the following summarizes its missions: "We provide comprehensive, high-quality group health care sharing plans to manage all your health care needs and protect you from unexpected high medical expenses. This cost-effective alternative to health insurance grants you more freedom and control over the way you wish to receive care." The company offers plans for one-person businesses, individuals, and families as well as group memberships for businesses up to 49 full-time equivalent employees.

According to the company's website, MPB.Health stands out from the competition because it "is the only non-insurance-based, low-cost health care solution available today offering a variety of health plan options that include a full array of services to manage all your health care needs," such as:

Telehealth 24/7/365
Medical Cost Sharing
Minimal Essential Coverage (MEC as per the Affordable Care Act)
Life Care for Mental Health and Life/Work Assistance
Complementary and Alternative Medicine (CAM) Discount Network
Cost and Quality Search for Procedures, Labs, Imaging and More
Pharmacy Program
QR Life Code for ER
MPB Concierge Services M-F

Source: https://mpb.health/groups/

MPB.Health memberships pair well with direct primary care (DPC) providers, health savings accounts (for memberships including the MEC), and health matching accounts to give members ongoing support physically and to help provide the upfront costs financially. MPH.Health memberships give members a full array of services and benefits for most health care needs. Expert advisors guide clients on the best solutions and best practices for each individual or group.

Conclusion

Physician/entrepreneurs and nonphysician entrepreneurs are offering businesses another option to provide health care for their employees that is affordable, transparent, and increases choices for individuals and their families. A cost-sharing arrangement may be just what the doctor ordered to tackle the high cost of traditional insurance that is making small business, in some cases, less competitive in attracting talent. For large companies, which have more bargaining power with the big insurance companies, it behooves them to add to the bottom line without reducing employees' benefits. In fact, a cost-sharing arrangement for large companies could make them super attractive to talent that wants more control over their medical benefits. In short, a cost-sharing arrangement may be the win–win solution that both employers and employees desire.

As we have seen in Chapter 1, a company's culture will dictate, to a large degree, what employees will embrace to keep both morale and productivity high. For employers who would be considering a cost-sharing arrangement, representatives from faith-based and secular organizations should be invited to first speak with the human resource personnel to educate them about the strengths and opportunities of this option. If the HR folks are amenable to the idea of having employees learn about cost sharing, then I suggest depending on the size of the workforce, small groups over the course of several days during a lunch hour listen to the cost-sharing structure of each of several companies. Small groups would allow more interaction between employees and cost-sharing representatives. When it comes to a new idea about health care, employers must allay any concerns that their workforce would be worse off in a cost-sharing arrangement.

The future of employer-based insurance will have to be based on innovation and thinking "out of the box." A cost-sharing arrangement probably has not been considered by most employers because they are either unaware of its existence or heard negative comments or remarks, from others. The best advice for entrepreneurs would be to do their due diligence to determine if cost sharing has a role to play in their employees' benefits package.

CHAPTER 9

Lessons From Abroad

According to one poll, only 30 percent of the American people are very satisfied or fairly satisfied with health care while another 25 percent are neither satisfied nor dissatisfied. And not surprisingly 43 percent of Americans are not very or not at all satisfied with health care.[1]

What accounts for this dismal assessment of America's health care system? In a recent essay,[2] Robert H. Shmerling, MD, highlights what physicians, nurses, economists and other social scientists, public officials, employers, employees, and the insured and anyone else that pays for or needs medical care generally acknowledge. The U.S. medical care system (a term I prefer to use instead of health care) is expensive, opaque, and bureaucratic. The American people spend more on medical care as a percentage of GDP than any other nation and yet "the US scores poorly in many key health measures, including life expectancy, preventable positions, suicide, and maternal mortality."[3] A contentious issue that has been addressed by legislation is surprise billing, that is, when a patient gets a bill from an anesthesiologist, for example, because he was not in his network and had no idea what his services would cost, it will no longer devastate a family's budget (see www.cms.gov/nosurprises/Ending-Surprise-Medical-Bills).

Some (many?) critics decry the "health care disparities" in our country, because low-income individuals and families, especially minority households, do not have the same "access" to medical care as the majority of Americans. In addition, insurance companies have a tendency to deny coverage for medically necessary care to hold down costs, which is self-defeating, because it could lead to more expensive procedures or the need for more potentially costly medication in the future.

Another critique is that America's medical care system focuses on treating diseases rather than assisting patients to stay healthy. As Shmerling recounts, "During my medical training, I received relatively little instruction in nutrition, exercise, mental health, and primary care, but plenty of time was devoted to inpatient care, intensive care units, and subspecialties such as cardiology and gastroenterology."[4] In addition, medical care "overemphasizes procedures and drugs." This means a cortisone injection for tendinitis typically is covered by insurance but a shoe insert that may be a better solution may not be.[5]

Another shortsighted approach to medical care is the "stifling of innovation." Many patients would prefer to receive medical treatment at home, all other things being equal, instead of in a hospital. The COVID-19 pandemic increased the use of telemedicine that now has become a routine approach to medical care.[6]

Shmerling cites other factors that drive up costs and impact patients adversely. Malpractice lawsuits escalate insurance costs, which tend to be passed on to employers and employees in the form of higher insurance premiums or fees. In addition, "fragmented care," according to Shmerling, reduces the coordination of best practices, causing patients to not receive the highest quality care they need to treat their illness or disease.[7] However, with electronic records being the standard method of collecting patient data, one would think this should not be an issue, as physicians should have access to patients' drug prescriptions, test results, and other vital information.

Nevertheless, what is the solution(s) to America's medical care challenges that Shmerling and others have identified so that all the stakeholders, primarily patients, get affordable quality care where prices are transparent, waiting times are minimized, and access is virtually universal?

A March 2021 poll reveals that 55 percent of Americans support "Medicare for All," a single-payer system, where all medical care would be paid for by the government, that is, it would be a taxpayer-funded system and there would be no private insurance; 32 percent oppose such an approach. This so-called public option is supported by 68 percent of the voters and has broad support from both Democrats and Republicans.[8] With health care costs being a major concern for families in virtually all income groups and seniors, according to a Kaiser Family Foundation (KKF) poll,[9] it is not surprising legislators, physicians, and others are looking to health care systems around the world where government involvement is greater than in the United States or mandates are an integral component of universal coverage.

I have surveyed several foreign medical care systems. They include the single-payer systems of Canada, England, and Taiwan, and the universal health care systems of Switzerland, Singapore, Germany, and the Nordic countries. None of them are "pure," in the sense that their citizens do have options such as supplemental policies or they can pay for a portion of their medical costs out of pocket. In addition, these government medical care systems are not "free." Taxpayers, who bear the burden to fund the "free" government programs, pay for the cost of their medical care. In other words, there is no "free lunch" when it comes to governments funding any program.

In this chapter, I will briefly review the single-payer systems and universal medical care systems cited above. They each have their unique components and I will highlight their strengths and weaknesses so you can see how medical care is delivered and paid for in nations that have more of a "top-down" approach. If there are any lessons from abroad about how to structure a medical care system that would be applicable to America's culture and political and economic reality, then employers may decide that unburdening themselves from health care decisions for their employees may make sense. They, in turn, could make the case to their legislators that America too needs to abandon employer-based insurance.

Single-Payer Systems

Canada

Although I have placed Canada in the single-payer category, the country could just as easily be identified as an example of universal medical care. Nevertheless, the perception among many Americans is that Canada's single-payer system should be emulated and therefore is the primary reason I included it in this category.

As Senator Bernie Sanders, a two-time presidential candidate, remarked, "In Canada, for a number of decades, they have provided quality care to people without out-of-pocket expenses. You go in for cancer therapy, you don't take out your wallet."[10] Sanders' perception is that virtually all medical care costs would be paid for by the government and that the costs would be reasonable, with no adverse consequences, either in quality of care, undue waiting time to receive treatment, or access to specialists. So what is the reality of the Canadian health care system?

In reality, Canada's public (taxpayer) funded system (Canadian Medicare) is decentralized and funded by the country's 13 provinces and territories (P/T). The P/Ts run their own insurance plans and the federal government chips in with funds as well. Health care is provided to citizens and permanent residents in the form of hospital and physician services "free of charge." There are, however, excluded services such as outpatient prescription drugs and dental care, but the P/Ts cover some of the costs for "targeted groups." Despite "free" health care provided by the government, about two out of three Canadians also purchase private insurance, which covers excluded services such as vision, dental care, outpatient prescription drugs, rehabilitation services, and private hospital rooms. Patients pay out of pocket; they have their own insurance; or their employers pay for private insurance.[11]

Physicians are typically in private practice and self-employed, and patients can choose their general physician (GP). Provincial ministries and their respective medical associations negotiate the fees for physicians. Most physicians and specialists bill the P/T governments directly and others are salaried staff of a hospital or facility. There are public and private hospitals, both profit and nonprofit.[12]

This general overview of the Canadian system reveals that it is more of a hybrid approach to medical care, involving both public and private institutions and private practice physicians, rather than a "pure" single-payer system. For Senator Sanders, some members of Congress, other health care analysts, and the America-based physicians who call for a National Health Plan, the Canadian model does not go far enough. American single-payer advocates want to eliminate all private insurance and have government-run medical care, in other words, Medicare for All, where everyone would be covered for all services, including prescription drugs and so on.

What then is the reality of the Canadian health care experience? According to economist Peter St. Onge's review of the Canadian health care system,

> Canadians bear similar medical out-of-pocket burdens as Americans, while paying far higher taxes. Lower overall health spending in Canada is largely achieved by rationing care with waiting lists, using cheaper drugs, skimping on equipment, and underinvesting in medical facilities and staff to the point of nationwide shortages. Far from the feel-good "we're all in this together" rhetoric, Canadian health care hides costs by throwing burdens on already suffering patients.[13]

Moreover, Canadian radiologist Lee Kurisko who moved to the United States after being a staunch supporter of his home country's health care system writes about the preventable deaths he witnessed because of the dysfunctional universal medical care system he participated in. As a matter of conscience and being devoted to the Hippocratic oath, he decided he could no longer be part of a medical care system that did not put patients first.[14] In short, Kurisko warns Americans to be careful in embracing a single-payer or universal medical care system.

England

The National Health Service (NHS) was created in 1948, and at the time, it was a model of a single-payer, universal medical care system. All citizens are covered with "free" physician and mental health services and hospitalization. Europeans who have a Health Insurance Card are eligible to receive free care. Others such as non-European visitors or undocumented immigrants can get free emergency care and treatment for some infectious diseases. Funds are provided mostly from general taxation. ("Free" medical care is thus a misnomer; patients pay indirectly for care with higher taxes.) Nearly 11 percent of the population carries private supplementary insurance for quicker access to elective care. As many as 191 Clinical

Commissioning Groups (CCG) oversee medical care, which is delivered at the local level, and pay for allowable expenses.[15]

The NHS covers or pays for a comprehensive list of services such as:[16]

- Preventive services, including screenings, immunizations, and vaccination programs
- Inpatient and outpatient hospital care
- Maternity care
- Physician services
- Inpatient and outpatient drugs
- Clinically necessary dental care
- Some parts of eye care
- Mental health care, including some care for those with learning disabilities
- Palliative care
- Some long-term care
- Rehabilitation, including physiotherapy (such as after-stroke care)
- Home visits by community-based nurses
- Wheelchairs, hearing aids, and other assistive devices for those assessed as needing them.

Reproduced with courtesy of the Commonwealth Fund.
Source: www.commonwealthfund.org/international-health-policy-center/countries/england

Local CCGs determine how these services will be delivered and most importantly how much will be paid for annually. In addition, there are out-of-pocket expenses, approximately 15 percent of total expenditures, which primarily is used for long-term care. The NHS covers 90 percent of drug prescriptions. Primary care doctors (GPs) act as "gatekeepers" for additional care and referrals to a specialist. Nearly 60 percent of GPs are self-employed, and doctors' fees are negotiated between the British Medical Association and the government. There is a shortage of GPs and medical education is highly regulated and guided by the government.

Hospitals are either publicly owned or private and operate as for-profit or nonprofit institutions.[17]

Costs are contained by a national care budget, which is set on a three-year cycle. Nevertheless, budget deficits have occurred and waiting times have increased, leading to the deteriorating quality of care.[18]

The NHS has existed for nearly three-quarters of a century. Its track record is no secret and thus an assessment of its strengths and weaknesses should be obvious to English citizens as well as analysts from diverse disciplines. Tim Evans, Professor of Business and Political Economy at Middlesex University, London, who is also a Senior Fellow with the Adam Smith Institute, has made an extensive assessment of the NHS. The main takeaways of his analysis are:[19]

- By 2023 the NHS budget will gobble up 38 percent of all UK government spending.
- The NHS does a relatively poor job in preventing deaths from heart attacks, strokes, cancer, and lung diseases. The number of doctors per capita in the UK is the lowest in the European Union.
- Waiting lists have been skyrocketing in the past decade.
- Funding increases and so-called reforms implemented in recent years have not eliminated bureaucratic overhead.
- Lastly, more citizens are seeking health care from private doctors, dentists, hospitals, nursing homes, and other non-government alternatives. In short, a "mixed" health care system is emerging in Britain, revealing the weaknesses of the top-down approach to medicine.

Source: www.commonwealthfund.org/international-health-policy-center/countries/england

Although the UK spends almost half of what the United States spends as a percentage of GDP, life expectancy has increased by more than 10 years since the NHS was created in 1948. In addition, infant mortality has declined precipitously; women spend less than two days in the hospital after giving birth, down from 14 days in 1948. A vaccination program launched in 1958 helped reduce the incidence of polio and diphtheria.[20]

Evans concludes his analysis of the NHS with these words:[21]

> Overall, Britain's experience with the NHS portends a number of lessons that American policymakers can apply as they consider the future of the U.S. health care system. Even with widespread electoral support and ever-increasing amounts of government expenditure, those who require medical treatment often end up suffering because of perpetual access problems. Although medicine and technology have advanced hugely around the world in recent decades, the British experience with socialized medicine is that it leads to comparatively poor outcomes...

The British experiment of national health care has been evolving since 1948 and the distortion, namely, the waiting time to see a specialist, is still a major flaw as well the apparent needless premature deaths from diseases and illnesses. Consequently, citizens are finding solutions in the marketplace for health care and "voting" with their pounds accordingly.

Nevertheless, is there a single-payer system that American policy makers and citizens can embrace to implement universal coverage and lower the world's highest medical care costs as a percentage of GDP? Is the relatively newly created Taiwan single-payer system the solution?

Taiwan

In 1995 after nearly eight years of planning and 18 months of legislative discussion, the island of Taiwan created a single-payer system, the National Health Insurance (NHI). Within the first year of operation, 90 percent of 21 million Taiwanese residents were enrolled.

The three pillars of Taiwan's system are as follows: (1) controlling costs by the government dictating prices; (2) "equity" in access, covered benefits, and "fairness" in financial contributions; and (3) reduced administrative costs. As a health policy research analyst, Tsung-Mei Chen (whose late husband, Princeton health care economist Uwe Reinhardt, was the architect of the Taiwan system) asserts in her overview of the

Taiwan system, "The NHI's sparkling performance over a quarter-century in terms of cost control, universal coverage and superior health outcomes makes clear that Taiwan made the right choice."[22]

What is the evidence that Taiwan is the model the United States should emulate to have better health outcomes and lower costs?

Taiwan spends just 6.4 percent of its GDP on health care well below the United States (19.7 percent in 2020), and is substantially lower than all modern, industrialized nations in the OECD (Organization for Economic Co-operation and Development). This is a major plus for the cost of health care in any nation. Other points made about the success of the NHI are mandatory enrollment regardless of preexisting conditions, quality monitoring by the NHIA, an IT system that reduces costs to less than 1 percent of the NHI budget, generous subsidies for low-income residents to pay premiums, and equal access to health care services. Doctors are in private practice and most hospitals are privately owned. Clinics are primarily private.[23]

Although a single-payer system is usually based on tax revenue to pay for health care, Taiwan chose a premium-based payment approach, where the revenue comes from employers, the government, and the insured. A payroll tax of 4.69 percent supplies 81 percent of NHI's revenue, almost evenly split between employers and the insured. A non-payroll premium provides 8 percent, subsidies from general government revenue cover 9 percent, and another 2 percent comes from a tobacco tax and lottery winnings.[24]

Taiwanese do not have long wait times for health care. For example, wait times (2015) for major surgeries were shorter than in Australia, Canada, Finland, the Netherlands, England, or Scotland, and no referrals or prior authorizations are required. In addition, health care competition is alive and well in the island nation. Instead of prices, which are set by the government, driving competition, doctors and hospitals compete for patients by providing better quality services. Patients have a full range of services—for which there are co-pays and coinsurance—that are covered by the NHI, including "inpatient and outpatient care, prescription drugs, dental care, Chinese medicine, renal dialysis, prenatal care, child delivery, physical rehabilitation, home nursing care, chronic mental health care, preventive services such as pediatric and adult check-ups, immunizations and cancer screening."[25]

A November 2019 poll revealed a 90 percent satisfaction rate for the NHI. Providers, on the other hand, are more dissatisfied than patients for obvious reasons. The government controls their income and 43 percent complain about the global budget, which controls costs for each of the five medical sectors—hospitals, primary care, dental care, Chinese medicine, and renal dialysis.[26]

NIH's IT system is also cited as a major innovation and cost-containment phenomenon, helping keep costs way down and allowing medical providers access to patient's records to provide them with information to treat them more effectively. In addition, patients have Web-based access to data allowing them to obtain reliable information about providers.

Tsung-Mei Chung asserts in her conclusion: "Taiwan is the poster child for how a wellrun (sic) single-payer system can do the job efficiently and still enjoy high public satisfaction. Taiwanese regard the NHI as a national treasure and the guardian of social peace."[27] Although the Taiwan single-payer system is less than 30 years old, is it sustainable and can it be replicated in the United States, a diverse—ethnically, culturally, racially, and so on—country spanning more than 3.8 million square miles with a population more than 15 times greater than the nation island? To ask the latter question is to answer it, for all intents and purposes.

A critique of Taiwan's single-payer system by Siok Hui Leong makes several cogent points. While acknowledging the strengths of the Taiwan system, Leong cites a 2015 report by Tsung Me-Chung, which outlines the challenges of the single-payer system: "A budget deficit, an aging population, a rise in chronic diseases, questionable quality of care, disgruntled doctors and incessant public demand on Taiwan's medical services."[28] One of the "successes" of the Taiwan system is, according to Chiang Kuan-yu, the "huge expense of health professionals." Chiang who is affiliated with the Taiwan Medical Alliance for Labor Justice and Patient Safety states that medical professionals "are tired and burnt out." Workloads could reach as high as 100 hours per week for residents. He reports that doctors who want to increase their incomes "order diagnostic tests, do invasive medical procedures or schedule follow-up appointments," thus creating a "moral hazard" in the practice of medicine. One of the fallouts of setting doctors' fees is the migration of some doctors to Singapore and China.[29]

In sum, Taiwan has so far threaded the needle, so to speak, creating universal (mandatory) coverage at affordable prices with price controls and the use of premiums to pay for health care. In short, Taiwan's single-payer system is in reality a "top-down" hybrid system using coercion and market mechanisms to provide universal coverage. Whether the Taiwan model will exist by the time it turns 50 in 2045 remains to be seen given the aging of the population and other challenges it faces.

The next section will review several universal health care systems that have been praised for their coverage and quality of medical services.

Universal Health Care Systems

A universal health care system typically has the national government mandating coverage for all citizens. Many nations require their citizens to have some form of medical insurance. In the United States, the Affordable Care Act (ACA also known as Obamacare) was passed with a mandate with "teeth." Individuals and families would have to pay a penalty if they did not have insurance. The penalty was eliminated at the federal level at the end of 2018, but a handful of states and the District of Columbia still impose a penalty.[30] On the other hand, Medicare, created in 1965, is not mandatory, despite the perception that you must enroll in Part A (hospital insurance coverage) while Part B (doctor and other bills) has always been voluntary. However, if you don't enroll in Part A, Social Security benefits are forfeited.[31] Thus, Part A is a "soft" mandatory program.

In the next section, I will provide an overview of health care in the Nordic countries, Switzerland, Singapore, and Germany.

The Nordic Countries

Nordic countries—Iceland, Sweden, Norway, Finland, and Denmark—share a common health care structure, which covers their citizens with taxpayer funds. Patients receive health care without—or minimal—out-of-pocket costs. The three pillars of all the countries are access, treatment, and public health. Each nation has its own specific national or local-level approach to achieve these objectives. The World Health

Organization and numerous studies have cited the high level of health care outcomes in the region.[32]

The cost of universal care is funded by a combination of taxes (typically 75–85 percent of total costs), co-payments, and cost-sharing, especially for adult prescription drug needs. Patient payments are capped and low-income individuals with chronic conditions have these fees waived. Since the 1990s, more "flexibility" and patient choices have been implemented as long wait times even for serious illnesses have caused public dissatisfaction. Although health care costs have increased markedly in recent years, the Nordic countries still spend much less of their GDP on health care (8.5 percent in Iceland to 10.9 percent in Sweden) than the United States.[33]

Hospitals are under the umbrella of local or regional governments, and GPs are in private practice paid by a capitation fee and fees for services. They act as "gatekeepers" for the system. Salaries for hospital physicians and others are determined by collective bargaining agreements.[34]

Not surprisingly, the Nordic universal health care systems are facing challenges from an aging population, unhealthy lifestyles, and to some degree an influx of immigrants. Financing medical technology and the continued training of health care professionals to maintain competency is a concern because of limited budgets. To address rising costs, hospitals have consolidated and reduced stays markedly. To keep major medical costs under control, the emphasis on healthy lifestyles has been a major initiative throughout the Nordic countries.[35]

The challenges the Nordic countries face have led an increased demand for private insurance. In Denmark, Sweden, and Norway, private insurance is typically provided by employers and is used to supplement the government-run plan. Private insurance allows patients to gain faster access to specialists and elective procedures.[36] The counterpart in the United States would be a supplemental plan the seniors purchase to pay for expenses that Medicare does not cover.

Overall, the Nordic countries use tax dollars to provide medical care to their citizens, who grumble about high taxes and occasionally long waits to see a specialist. The bottom line is that while health care is universal in countries that have healthy populations, concern is raised about its outcomes. Are outcomes a result of universal care in the Nordic countries or in spite of it?

Switzerland

The Swiss universal care model is straightforward. All citizens are required to purchase medical coverage through "government-approved nonprofit insurance providers." The Swiss Federal Law on Health Insurance regulates the insurance companies to make sure that "prices are fair and that all residents receive the same high-quality care." The 60+ providers offer the same coverage, which includes "illnesses, maternity care, accidents, and emergencies. Furthermore, home visits are covered by insurance in most cases. And services such as physiotherapy, nursing care, occupational therapy, speech therapy, and nutritional counseling are covered if your doctor recommends them."[37] The insurance companies must cover preexisting conditions. The insurance providers also sell supplemental policies for services not covered under the private insurance policy, which covers 80 to 90 percent of medical costs.[38]

The Swiss spend approximately 12 percent of GDP on health care, well below the U.S. figure of approximately 19 percent, but it is expensive and the highest of any European country. Patients are highly satisfied with their medical care and spend on average 10 percent of their salaries on health insurance.[39]

The bottom line of the Swiss universal coverage system is that it is grappling with issues we find in the United States and other nations: improving quality of care, greater transparency, promoting more self-responsibility, and having better coordination of care.[40]

For more details about the decentralized Swiss system, see "Switzerland," published by the Commonwealth Fund, www.commonwealthfund.org/ international-health-policy-center/countries/switzerland.

Singapore

Singapore's health care system is one of the highest ranked in the world. Why? Its outcomes are generally considered superb. Health care is mandatory and is financed by a combination of taxes and private payments. There are three components of the Singapore system: Medishield Life covers large hospital bills and approved outpatient services. Patients are responsible for premiums, deductibles, coinsurance, and any costs not covered by the plan. Government subsidies are available to qualified individuals. MediSave is a compulsory medical savings account, which can be used to pay for inpatient care and other outpatient services. Supplemental private insurance can be purchased to offset costs; employers may provide this benefit. MediFund is the government-funded safety net program for low-income Singaporeans who are unable to pay for out-of-pocket expenses.[41]

MediSave is funded by employee and employer contributions, ranging from 8 to 10.5 percent, depending on age. These funds are deposited in a tax-exempt account, earning 4 percent for 2022.

The government's objective is to use competition to increase efficiency and ensure high-quality medical care to all their citizens. At just 4.5 percent of GDP spent on health care, Singapore currently has an envious low-cost, high-quality care system. The country has achieved its success with "strong government control and oversight." Using both market forces—fees for services—and a robust public sector to "guide" health care with subsidies and mandates, Singapore is in effect a hybrid system that provides universal coverage.

In the final analysis, could the Singapore model offer any lessons for the United States to create universal coverage that would relieve both employers and employees of the highest health care costs in the world? We will explore this in the next chapter about the future of medical insurance.

Germany

Chancellor Otto von Bismarck established Germany's national health insurance in 1883. Initially, health insurance modestly began covering only 10 percent of the population. Today, 88 percent are enrolled in the nonprofit statutory health insurance plan (SHI). So-called sickness funds are comparable to our insurance companies administering the plan. Funds for the SHI come from a 14.6 percent tax on wages and an average 1 percent supplemental "contribution" is also assessed. Both employers and employees pay taxes equally. Individuals have co-pays for inpatient services and drugs and the sickness funds apply to various deductibles. The wage contributions are then pooled into a national fund and distributed to individual sickness funds based on age, sex, and morbidity factors. The list of services covered by SHI ranges from preventive services including dental checkups, inpatient and outpatient hospital care, and a wide range of benefits including prescription drugs and sick leave compensation.[42]

Employees who earn more than $68,000 annually can purchase private insurance instead of enrolling in the SHI. A risk-based premium makes it attractive for young, healthy workers with high incomes. These workers can obtain more services with lower premiums. In addition, Germany has mandatory long-term insurance (LTCI) plan requirements.[43]

Although the federal government regulates health care with a range of rules, it does not provide care directly, which is left to private practitioners, who cannot charge more than the contracted fee schedule. The 2,500 clinics provide multispecialty services where doctors receive a salary. Public hospitals provide about half the beds in the country, and nonprofits account for about a third. Hospital physicians are salaried and are similar to the U.S. hospital physicians.

The bottom line about the German approach is straightforward: "The public health care system in Germany is distinguished for its generosity. All people insured by a public health insurer receive the same medical care regardless of their financial status. This is achieved through an income-based common fund…"

For nearly 120 years, the German health care system has been a model for mandatory public insurance with an option for private insurance for individuals above a certain income threshold. The health outcomes have been considered one of the best in the world with the country spending 12.5 percent of its GDP on health (2020).

Are there lessons for America given the substantial government involvement in overseeing the health care sector? At first glance, the German model would be appealing to employers because they would not have to contract with an insurance company to cover their employees. Employees would be enrolled in a sickness fund. However, employers would still have to pay into the sickness funds, as would their employees.

The Commonwealth Fund compared the health care systems of 11 high-income countries in a 2021 study (see Figure 9.1).

Using 71 performance metrics across five domains, the United States is ranked last, while Canada—a model for some American analysts and public officials—is ranked just ahead of our country. The highest ranked nations are two Nordic countries, Norway and the Netherlands, while

	AUS	CAN	FRA	GER	NETH	NZ	NOR	SWE	SWIZ	UK	US
OVERALL RANKING	3	10	8	5	2	6	1	7	9	4	11
Access to Care	8	9	7	3	1	5	2	6	10	4	11
Care Process	6	4	10	9	3	1	8	11	7	5	2
Administrative Efficiency	2	7	6	9	8	3	1	5	10	4	11
Equity	1	10	7	2	5	9	8	6	3	4	11
Health Care Outcomes	1	10	6	7	4	8	2	5	3	9	11

Figure 9.1 Ranking of health care systems in selected countries

Data: Commonwealth Fund analysis.
Source: Eric C. Schneider et al., Mirror, Mirror 2021—Reflecting Poorly: Health Care in the U.S. Compared to Other High-Income Countries (Commonwealth Fund, August 2021). https://doi .org/10.26099/01DV-H208.

Sweden ranks seventh. Although Taiwan and Singapore were not included in this study, they both received high marks in other comparisons, with Taiwan ranked #2 in the world by the World Population Review. Nevertheless, top-rated Commonwealth Fund countries were kept on a lower ranking by numerous studies, revealing the differing methodologies used to collect national data about costs, performance, efficiency, and outcomes.

The bottom line for our purposes here is what are the takeaways regarding lessons from abroad. The Singapore system would be hugely attractive to Americans because it potentially could reduce medical care costs by at least two-thirds and provide better outcomes for patients. That is the conclusion of the economist Sean Masaki Flynn's *The Cure That Works: How to Have the World's Best Healthcare—at a Quarter of the Price.* Flynn visited Singapore, toured its health care system, and praised it as the model the United States should emulate. The major pushback in the United States would be the mandatory purchase of medical insurance for the whole population; other government regulations put bureaucrats in charge of various medical care statutes. Otherwise, the Singapore model could be embraced by a majority of Americans who are frustrated by the current expensive hybrid system we have.

The next chapter will outline how employers can reduce their medical insurance costs not by lobbying for grand reforms at the federal and state levels but by implementing the alternatives that medical entrepreneurs have created in the past few years. In short, we do not have to look abroad for solutions to expensive and opaque medical insurance and care when the solutions are right here in the United States.

CHAPTER 10

The Future of Health/ Medical Insurance

Health insurance is the term used to describe the employer-based benefit that pays our medical bills. Health insurance is a misnomer. It should be called medical insurance, because when we are ill or have a disease, we need the services of a physician or other medical provider—such as a surgeon to become healthy. Medical insurance thus helps pay our bills for the services of a physician, surgeon, or a hospital stay, which can run into the tens, if not hundreds, of thousands of dollars. But as we shall see in this chapter, the cost of medical care can be reduced substantially and reduce, if not eliminate, the need for the current exorbitantly expensive hospitalizations and other medical expenses. Yes, there is a light at the end of the tunnel. In other words, there is a *revolution* occurring in the medical care sector despite the rules, regulations, and other roadblocks that are keeping "health care"[1] prices unconscionably high, which is the primary cause of personal bankruptcy in America.

Why has obtaining medical care become so complicated, expensive, and difficult to navigate?[2] Think about this, every year Americans of all ages, incomes, and education levels buy millions of new and used automobiles without the slightest knowledge of all the intricacies of engines, transmissions, and all the software that make motor vehicles run. Yet, even without this knowledge, the American people seamlessly purchase hundreds of billions of dollars of motor vehicles annually, because the public can do the research online to obtain expert opinions from Consumer Reports, Edmunds and Kelly Blue Book, to make informed choices.

But when it comes to medical care, the medical/health care experts tell us there are "asymmetries" in the medical sector and therefore the public cannot make an informed decision. In other words, the public does not have the same information as physicians and hospitals. Why should this be? The simple answer is the lack of transparency in purchasing medical care from physicians and hospitals. And from employees' perspectives, the reliance on employer-based insurance to get their bills paid makes them relatively "immune" from physicians' fees—except for co-pays deductibles—and hospital charges such as the $10 aspirin tablet. Therefore, the way we pay for our medical bills violates a fundamental economic principle, namely, in a market transaction between a willing buyer (in this case a patient) and the supplier (a physician or hospital) transparency makes possible the ability of the buyer to judge the value of the service being rendered or the goods being purchased. And by focusing on *value, the buyer perceives* a robust, competitive, and transparent market emerging for goods and services. The good news for both employers and employees is that we are headed in that direction for the "consumption" of medical care. Thus, medical care will be more affordable in the future and give consumers greater choices finally.

Restoring the Doctor–Patient Relationship

One of the first issues that need to be addressed in providing affordable medical care is to restore the doctor–patient relationship. William E. Bennett Jr., MD, makes this point in a 2019 essay, "Insurance Companies Aren't Doctors. So Why Do We Keep Letting Them Practice Medicine?"[3] Bennett, a gastroenterologist, reveals he has to submit "prior authorizations" to insurance companies for tests and expensive medications, if warranted, for his patients. Usually, the insurance company approves coverage after he speaks with a doctor or pharmacist working for the carrier. "What a waste of time," complains Bennett, because he could better be spending his time treating patients rather than speaking with a health care specialist to get an approval. But Bennett is not finished revealing his frustration with insurance companies. As he describes his experiences, "On most occasions the 'peer reviewer' is unqualified to make an assessment about the specific services his patients require. They usually have minimal or incorrect information about the patient. Not one has examined or spoken with the patient, as I have. None of them has a long-term relationship with the patient and family, as I have .... The insurance company will say this system makes sure patients get the right medications. It doesn't. It exists so that many patients will fail to get the medications they need."[4]

Bennett's suggestion would undoubtedly restore the doctor–patient relationship and cut out the "middleman," who is making medical decisions "without accepting the professional, personal or legal liability that comes with the territory."[5] He concludes his essay by declaring what is generally considered one of the great flaws in American medicine and a common-sense solution: "Health care in the United States is shockingly opaque; it's time to take the insurance companies out of our decision-making process."[6]

Transparent Pricing

If transparency is one of the keys to affordable medical care and if market transactions between buyers and sellers should be the means by which patients and health care providers get together, then the Free Market Medical Association (FMMA.org) is in the vanguard of the *medical care revolution*. Founded in 2014 by Jay Kempton, Owner, The Kempton Group Administrators and Dr. Keith Smith, Medical Director, Surgery Center of Oklahoma, FMMA's mission is to promote transparency in health care, make health care affordable, and bring buyers and sellers together.

On the About page, the following statements highlight the organization's objectives.[7]

> The free market movement in healthcare is gaining steam. This is because of providers, patients, and self-funded employers, who believe that changing the way we purchase healthcare services is necessary, and seeking out value driven healthcare providers is important.
>
> Matching a willing buyer with a willing seller of valuable healthcare services is the goal of everyone involved in this movement. We help identify patients willing to pay cash, doctors willing to list their prices, businesses attempting to provide affordable quality insurance, and providers/services/and patient advocates that are helping make everything work.

For a transparent medical care market to be implemented, FMMA has constructed three pillars of free-market medicine—price, value, and equality. As far as the price pillar is concerned, FMMA points out care is the product, not price. According to FMMA, the current insurance arrangements that employers rely on to provide medical care to their employees raise costs and thus should be replaced by cash payments. When buyers and sellers agree on a price and the process has been transparent, then the *value pillar has been established*. And when cash buyers are "customers" of medical care, the price should be offered to all thus establishing the pillar of *equality*. In short, "In a free market system, a competitive price can be knowable, publishable, and complete regardless of the patient."[8]

Dr. Smith's experience in creating the Surgery Center of Oklahoma (SCO) led him to incorporate the three *pillars* of free-market medicine. In doing so, he and his colleagues at SCO have reduced the cost of medical care, revealing the gross overcharging by hospitals and traditional medical practices, thereby inflating the cost of medical insurance.

Surgery Center of Oklahoma

Doctors Keith Smith and Steve Lantier founded the Surgery Center of Oklahoma (SCO) in April 1997. They created the cash-only clinic after they became disenchanted with their hospital anesthesia practices. As Smith recounts in his talk at the Mises Institute Medical Freedom Summit in June 2021, "… hospitals were awful and inefficient places charging patients gigantic prices."[9] Instead of butting heads with administrators, he and his partner became medical entrepreneurs to provide patients better quality medical care, lower prices, and give physicians the opportunity to practice medicine without insurance companies or bureaucrats interfering with the doctor–patient relationship.

The SCO quickly brought into the fold so to speak surgeons with whom both Smith and Lantier had an amicable working relationship. As the SCO's reputation grew in the community, patients flocked to Tulsa to get needed surgery at a deeply discounted price.

Dr. Smith describes one of his first patients without insurance who wanted a breast mass removed and how his center did the procedure for

$1,900 including a pathologist's report. The patient was quoted $19,000 by the local hospital for just facility, a ten-fold amount higher than the SCO!

Despite providing quality, affordable medical care, hospitals were outraged that they had a competitor, which in effect exposed their highly exorbitant prices. Insurance companies would pay the SCO as an out-of-network provider, but under pressure from hospitals, the insurers became hostile to Smith and Lantier's new project. Nevertheless, the SCO has thrived despite the medical establishment's opposition, but thankfully it had allies in the state legislature who supported the center's transparent, affordable, and high-quality model of medical care (all prices are posted online, surgerycenterok.com). Many legislators did not succumb to the hospitals' lobbying efforts to put roadblocks in SCO's way.

The SCO's impact has been nothing short of phenomenal as Dr. Smith explained in his address.[10]

> While there are many examples of money saved [for] uninsured individuals, one that sticks out is the patient from Georgia who required a urologic procedure, and who had received a quote of $40,000, just for the facility charge. A friend had told him about our facility and after he confirmed that our all-inclusive price was $4,000, he informed his urologist he was traveling to Oklahoma City. Having lost another patient to us the previous month, the urologist contacted the hospital and told them something had to be done, as their price quotes were causing him to lose patients. The hospital matched our price and the patient stayed in Georgia. The patient later told me that we had saved him $36,000 and we hadn't even performed his surgery.

This is more evidence that the costs of hospital surgeries are grossly inflated. That a hospital and surgeon were willing to match SCO's price speaks volumes about the current egregious anticompetitive practices prevalent in the traditional medical care sector.

If surgeons and hospitals throughout the country could match the SCO's price structure, then the annual cost of surgical procedures could decline by hundreds of billions. Employers could capture those savings (a greater bottom line) and employees could obtain higher wages and salaries. Moreover, employees may opt for additional nonmedical benefit, such as tuition assistance for their children.

In summing up his remarks at the Mises Institute Medical Summit, Dr. Smith is optimistic about the future because a more market-based environment has been emerging and is growing, and delivering efficient, value-based medical care. For that reason, employers have choices, as do uninsured employees, to customize their needs and pocketbook to obtain medical care using the resources provided by the above organizations or any other company that is using market principles to provide alternatives to traditional health care insurance.

Self-Insuring

Without a doubt, employees desire comprehensive medical insurance for themselves and their families as part of an employer's compensation package. This is completely reasonable given the cost of medical care in the country. For many years, employer-based medical insurance was straightforward. Employers contacted an insurance broker who typically represented one or more carriers to purchase a group policy for their employers. However, with insurance premiums rising steadily for decades, employers have become frustrated enough to seek alternatives to traditional medical insurance.

For the decade ending in 2020, insurance premiums rose 47 percent and deductibles jumped nearly 69 percent. That increase is more than double the general rise in prices over the period. In short, insurance premiums are a huge burden for both employers and employees, who paid on average nearly $6,000 toward their employers' average $22,221 for family coverage.[11]

Nearly 155 million workers get medical insurance from their employers, and about 50 percent of Americans are covered by employer-based insurance. Employees lacking employer based medical insurance have an option, subsidized private insurance if they qualify through the federal health exchange (healthcare.gov) or a state exchange.[12] Thus, the Affordable Care Act, aka Obamacare, has made medical insurance accessible for tens of millions of Americans. The pros and cons of Obamacare are beyond the scope of this section but are discussed briefly in Chapter 4. There are a huge number of studies about Obamacare. A Google search of the pros and cons resulted in more than 3.5 million hits. Happy reading!

Nevertheless, Chapters 4–8 review how medical insurance and health care coverage have evolved. Initially, traditional indemnity policies were the most common coverage employers would purchase to make sure their employees could be assured that virtually all their health care expenses would be paid for. This arrangement made employees secure that they were not one major illness away from financial ruin for themselves and their family members. For decades, this "contract" between employees and employers worked relatively well. But with medical care inflation and the resulting skyrocketing cost of medical insurance premiums, employers have become more "proactive" in purchasing medical insurance. Instead of being "price takers," more and more employers have been cutting out the insurance companies by self-insuring.

In 1999, self-insured plans covered 44 percent of employees. That number rose to 67 percent in 2020 and then declined to 64 percent in 2021.[13] In addition, at America's largest companies, 82 percent of employees are covered totally or partially by self-insured plans.[14] Employers have been voting with their dollars by opting out of the traditional medical insurance market.

Should your company consider a self-funding plan? What are the benefits for you and your employees and what are the downsides?

By opting for a self-insured plan, employers do not have to pay state insurance premium taxes and are not be subject to state-mandated coverage requirements, which allows them to customize employee insurance coverage. However, "self-insured group health plans come under all applicable federal laws, including the Employee Retirement Income Security Act (ERISA), Health Insurance Portability and Accountability Act (HIPAA), Consolidated Omnibus Budget Reconciliation Act (COBRA), the Americans with Disabilities Act (ADA), the Pregnancy Discrimination Act, the Age Discrimination in Employment Act, the Civil Rights Act, and various budget reconciliation acts such as Tax Equity and Fiscal Responsibility Act (TEFRA), Deficit Reduction Act (DEFRA), and Economic Recovery Tax Act (ERTA)."[15]

Depending on your company's demographics and culture, a self-funded plan could include benefits your employees would like to see covered, such as dental, vision, prescription drugs, and other expenses, such as chiropractic or acupuncture treatments. Furthermore, wellness programs to lower medical care costs could be just what the doctor ordered, explaining to employees that reducing medical claims would put money into their pockets, and give them additional vacation time or personal days. This would be a win–win for both employers and employees by sharing the decline in the costs of medical claims.[16] (For a contrary view of the efficacy of wellness programs, see Dave Chase's guide for employers available as a free download, https://healthrosetta.org/friends/#download.)

Another compelling reason for employers to self-insure is they have access to their employees' claim records, which should make it easier to forecast and plan future medical expenses. In addition to having a comprehensive "profile" of their employees' medical conditions, employers would then have an opportunity to introduce or expand wellness programs to control costs.[17]

Employees whose employers shift from a traditional plan to a self-funded plan would probably not see any change in their coverage. In fact, employees may not even notice any major change because they would retain their primary care physician and have access to specialists who may have arrangements with self-insured plans that could be more cost-effective for scores of employers in the community. In addition, to reduce administrative costs, medical bills would be sent to a third-party administrator (TPA) or sent to the company's benefits manager for payment. A TPA usually provides information to employees so they can navigate the medical benefits the plan allows, such as going to a clinic instead of a hospital for X-rays, MRIs and other tests that may in the past have been performed in an expensive hospital setting.[18]

As far as potential downsides, employers could cut back on benefits to reduce their overall medical care benefits. However, given the competitive labor market that has evolved since the COVID-19 epidemic, employers would have a hard time attracting workers up and down the organization with "skimpy" medical coverage unless they are creative with providing appealing overall benefits. This could be in the form of generous Health Savings Accounts.

Another potential shortcoming particularly for small businesses that self-insure is excessive claims. However, companies can purchase stop-loss insurance that will cap their liability.[19] For an informative FAQ about stop-loss insurance, see www.siia.org/i4a/pages/index.cfm?pageid=7535.

Alain C. Enthoven, emeritus professor of management (Stanford University), health care consultant and advisor to presidents, is a critic of self-insurance, who advocates a different approach to quality, affordable medical care.[20] His basic criticism is that "it has the effect of locking in uncoordinated, open-ended fee-for-service (FFS) and locking out comparatively economical Integrated Delivery Systems (IDS)."[21] What is an IDS?[22]

> An IDS is an organized, coordinated and collaborative network that links various health care providers, via common ownership or contract, to provide a coordinated continuum of services to a voluntarily enrolled patient population; the IDS is accountable, both clinically and fiscally, for the outcomes and health status of the population served, and has systems in place to manage and improve these outcomes. Typically, this means per capita prepayment, multi-specialty group practices, strong primary care, a focus on health promotion and disease prevention, and salaried doctors.

Enthoven asserts that an integrated approach to health care could reduce, if not eliminate, the estimated "30–40 percent of US health expenditures [that] are wasted—spending that does not improve the health of patients."[23] Many analysts would agree with Enthoven's assessment, but begs the question, namely are there current arrangements that would achieve his goals: increase quality, reduce costs, and improve the public's health and wellness? In addition, Enthoven recognizes that "some employers are achieving significant cost savings and quality gains by combining centers of excellence and bundled payments for complex procedures. But these programs are not scaled or common, and when they do exist, accessing such care is likely to mean travel from the patient's home. They also miss the mark in terms of the continuity of care."[24]

Nevertheless, Enthoven's "managed competition" model is another alternative to the current employer-based discussion that should be part of the public policy debate regarding medical care. Suffice it to say, employers are taking matters into their own hands and not waiting for regulatory changes to provide medical care for their employees.

Which Insurance Option Should an Employer Choose?

In the final analysis, employers have numerous combinations and permutations to consider for employee medical care insurance/arrangements. What are the side-by-side comparisons employers who are not self-insured have to choose from? Let's start from a top-down approach. The largest insurers by revenue are UnitedHealth Group, Anthem (Blue Cross and Blue Shield Companies), Centene, Kaiser Permanente, Humana, CVS Health (Aetna), Health Care Service Corp. (HSCS), and Molina Healthcare. The top five carriers by membership are UnitedHealth, Anthem. Aetna, Cigna, and Humana.[25] The top five companies by market share have nearly 46 percent of the national health insurance market. However, in some local markets, the Blues® may have as much as a 90 percent market share. (A point Dave Chase of Health Rosetta made to me in his review of this chapter.)

If employers choose one of the insurance "behemoths," that is one decision they have to make, but more decisions are necessary. The next decision is what type of insurance "network" is affordable and will give employees access to timely medical services (we all hate having to wait weeks or months to see a specialist or even a few days to see a primary care physician) and compassionate, quality care. Should an employer opt for an HMO, PPO (preferred provider organization), POS (point of service), or EPO (exclusive provider organization)? A general overview of all these plans and the "tiers" (Platinum, Gold, Silver, and Bronze) they offer can be found at www.medmutual.com/For-Individuals-and-Families/Health-Insurance-Education/Health-Insurance-Basics/Types-Health-Insurance.aspx#HMO.

Employers may also consider offering their employees a high-deductible health plan (HDHP) combined with and a Health Savings Account (HSA) or Health Reimbursement Account (HRA), which may be the ideal benefit for companies with young, healthy workers who would not need extensive—and expensive—medical care for years.[26] A crucial decision, therefore, for employers to attract and maintain a productive workforce is what health care benefits should they provide in the current competitive environment? A few suggestions in the next section on controlling costs—a key factor in a company's compensation package— would assist decision makers in both large and small businesses make an optimal choice regarding health care.

The Montana Experience: Market Forces at Work

Several years ago, the State of Montana hired Marilyn Bartlett, a 64-year-old grandmother and a former insurance executive, to fix its financially troubled self-insured plan. Bartlett's experience is a case study on how tough negotiations with hospitals throughout the state substantially reduced the fees. The state's self-insured plan was spiraling out of control because costs were rising markedly. Her tactics and strategies while not 100 percent applicable to small and medium-sized companies that want to cut their onerous hospital and drug costs down reveal the opaque way the medical care sector has operated for decades. Bartlett's "pushback" and how Montana—that is, the state's taxpayers—saved tens of millions of dollars, is a must-read for city and state government officials as well as CFOs of large companies who believe they have no choice but to continue to pay exorbitant hospital fees and high drug costs.[27]

If there is "strength in numbers," then small companies can create a consortium in their city, county, state, or region to "play hardball" with hospitals and drug companies. Companies could create a team of knowledgeable managers and work with a local business group such as a Chamber of Commerce to negotiate lower prices for their companies, and some, most, or all the savings could be used to increase wages and salaries. In other words, market forces are the best method to keep costs down and ensure transparency so buyers can determine the value of hospital services and other that of other providers. But as Dave Chase remarked in his feedback, sometimes small companies are at an advantage in dealing with hospital prices, because hospitals can be flexible in pricing their services to show they are "good local citizens."

Health Rosetta—Individual Wellness and Cost Reduction

The Seattle nonprofit outlines how inflated medical care costs have hurt workers' incomes and savings for decades, increased bankruptcies, hurt businesses' bottom lines, and ripped off taxpayers because of sky-high medical costs city, state, and federal governments have been paying. With that in mind, the nonprofit has a brief mission: "Healthcare has already been fixed. Our mission is to scale adoption of the fixes."[28]

For business owners and decision makers, Health Rosetta has created an Employer Program to help them reduce their health care costs by 20–40 percent or more, given that "It's estimated by organizations such as PwC and the Institute of Medicine that 30–50% of all health care spending is waste, fraud, or abuse. If health care is 20% of your payroll expenses, this is like a 6–10% perpetual payroll tax on your competitiveness."[29]

On Health Rosetta's Employer page, the following outline could help your company rein in health care costs.[30]

The Health Rosetta is made up of specific components and strategies that enable you to repeat what others have done.

While not exhaustive, here are a few major areas likely to have the quickest and most significant impact on reducing your total spend.

Components

1. Major Specialties and Outlier Patients
2. Transparent Pharmacy Benefits
3. Transparent Medical Markets
4. Transparent Independent Third Party Administrator
5. Payment Integrity

Strategies

1. Centers of Excellence networks
2. Reference-based pricing
3. Out-of-network claims settlement
4. Unbundling self-insured health plans

Note that all Health Rosetta components and strategies must be proven to reduce your spend, your employees' out-of-pocket spend, and improve the quality of care your employees receive.

Reproduced with permission of Dave Chase of Health Rosetta.

Health Rosetta (HR) points out improving employees' wellness is one of the keys to keeping medical costs down. Our medical care system is anything but that, according to HR, thus our system should focus on primary care and prevention. For example, Rosen Hotels & Resorts in Florida has been employing this approach for more than 30 years (with on-site health services, health coaches, nutritionists, and nurses) and has saved more than $500 million, which has been used to pay for employees and their children's college expenses. Employee turnover not surprisingly is 20 percent of the industry average.[31]

MPB Health

MPB.Health's mission is to provide resources so individuals and companies can bypass traditional medical insurance and take control of their costs and increase wellness for members. The all-inclusive plan MPB.Health offers include:[32]

- Medical cost sharing for protection from large medical expenses
- Telehealth services that allow you to communicate with a board-certified physician in minutes
- Mental health counseling and assistance with life and work challenges
- Preventive care and unlimited primary care with no office fees
- Pharmacy benefits plan
- Protection from medical expenses incurred overseas and all throughout the United States
- Personalized concierge support and assistance
- Health care discounts on alternative medical services (or integrative medicine, chiropractic, acupuncture, and massage therapy, as well as yoga, Pilates, gym memberships, and more!)
- Additional features include dental, vision, and health savings accounts

Source: https://mpb.health/groups/

To help employees pay for medical bills without "breaking the bank," MPB.Health highly recommends an Individual Coverage Health Reimbursement Arrangement (ICHRA), which was discussed in

Chapter 5. For both employees and employers who want to take control of their health care expenditures using an ICHRA, the benefits of such an account are obvious.[33]

Individual Coverage Health Reimbursement Arrangement (ICHRA) is an employer-funded, tax-advantaged health reimbursement arrangement. The employer sets aside a chosen amount of pre-tax dollars for their employees to pay for medical expenses. Moreover, ICHRA has no size restrictions and can be implemented with small businesses and large corporations. The employer can customize reimbursements with each class of employees, as well as have the freedom to choose what type of medical expenses are eligible for reimbursement.

In short, if more employers demand and opt for the model of health care Dr. Smith and his colleagues around the country have embraced—cash payment, Direct Primary Care, HSAs, ICHRAs, cost-sharing, and other arrangements—then it logically follows that the profession will have to become more entrepreneurial in response to market forces. It is up to employers who have been pummeled by rising medical insurance premiums to educate their employees about how everyone wins in the workplace if health care costs can be reduced by "thinking out of the box," namely, substituting proven market-based alternatives to expensive traditional medical insurance policies.

Notwithstanding the medical insurance maze that employers have to navigate to provide health care benefits to their employees, medical entrepreneurs are doing what they do best—creating and innovating to give employers insurance options. These options range from self-insuring, Direct Primary Care, concierge medicine, and cost-sharing arrangements. For the most part, these options restore the doctor–patient relationship, a critical component for every individual to reach optimal health. Instead of seeing a physician when an illness occurs, the focus of doctors such as Nate Favini of Forward is to replace our "sick care" system with an effective wellness care to prevent chronic illnesses and the high cost of treating these debilitating medical conditions.

With the advances in various screening tools, Artificial Intelligence, and blood tests, physicians are better able to assess an individual's genetic dispositions, lifestyle, and environmental factors to provide a roadmap for optimal health. Instead of treating symptoms of illnesses, the emerging paradigm is so to speak to nip chronic illnesses before a patient would need surgery, hospitalization, and one or more pharmaceutical protocols.

The employer-based medical insurance model will be with us for the time being as long as employees expect this perk to be an integral component of their compensation package. The options employers now have—and will have as medical care innovation continues—will improve a business's bottom line and give employees additional opportunities to improve their health with proven wellness programs. In addition, employers give their employees a medical care package where they can take more "ownership" of their medical choices bodes well for the future of employer-based medical care.

Appendix

The following sections contain information about substitutes for traditional health insurance. The challenge for business decision makers is to tailor a health insurance benefits package that will provide their employees with a cost-effective approach to obtain medical services. Understanding any health insurance policy is a daunting task even for knowledgeable human resource managers. Simplifying the contract between providers and employers would be one of the benefits of not enrolling employees in a traditional insurance policy or even a self-insurance plan. Thus, benefits managers and employees should be on the same page, so to speak, to have medical coverage that gives the workforce an easily understood contract, which includes a choice of physicians, few bureaucratic hurdles to jump over to see a specialist and access to quality medical care. Presenting medical coverage options that combine the best of market-based alternatives would enhance a company's ability to retain and attract talented employees.

Health Savings Accounts

The federal website contains basic information about HSAs and links to other sites to understand the IRS guidelines for offering them to your employees.

www.healthcare.gov/glossary/health-savings-account-hsa/

Fidelity® Investments has a comprehensive overview of its HSA, www .fidelity.com/go/hsa/why-has. Fidelity has received awards for its HSA.

Livelyme.com offers HSA resources for employers, https://livelyme .com/resources/employer/.

Millenialmoney.com ranks the best HSAs, https://millennialmoney. com/best-hsa-accounts/.

The above links should provide benefits managers with sufficient information to determine if a HSA that must be coupled with a high deductible plan is the best option for their companies.

Direct Primary Care

The Direct Primary Care Coalition would be a worthwhile place to begin finding out how DPC may be an alternative to typical physician services for your employees, www.dpcare.org. The website contains a national map with the locations of DPC physicians. At DPC Frontier, a state-by-state overview of the laws governing DPC practices is a vital tool that provides necessary information to sift through this maze.

There is an insufficient number of DPC physicians now available to serve an influx of tens of thousands of new patients. How can DPC practices be scaled to create hundreds if not thousands of new DPC physicians? Employers can form a recruitment consortium—locally, regionally or nationally—and ask DPC physicians to speak with medical students about becoming a DPC physician. An incentive for any medical student to become a DPC physician could be paying for part or all of their medical education and a bonus for opening a practice in the community.

Concierge Medicine Resources

At www.findmydirectdoctor.com/blogs/concierge-medicine-for-employers/af227c6f5e63bfbfc635ce5148e6c735 employers can learn why this medical coverage could be a good fit for their companies. And on this page, www.findmydirectdoctor.com/cm, employers and others can locate where to find concierge doctors by state, city, and specialty.

Cost-Sharing Arrangements

HSA for America has compiled a list of what it considers the best plans in the country, https://hsaforamerica.com/blog/the-hsa-for-america-healthshare-plan-comparison-2020-update/

At https://mpb.health, employers can evaluate the services this company offers that includes a cost-sharing arrangement. Also, clients acknowledge https://sedera.com, founded by Dr. Tony Dale, who began practicing medicine in the single payer English system, as a cost-effective alternative to traditional insurance.

For additional reviews of health sharing arrangements, see https://wellkeptwallet.com/health-sharing-plans/.

Case Studies of Employers Reducing Medical Care Expenses

- City of Milwaukee, https://f.hubspotusercontent40.net/hubfs/481991/Relocalizing%20Health%20Book/Split%20chapters%20and%20Case%20studies/Split%20case%20studies/City%20of%20Milwaukee.pdf
- Copper State Bolt & Nut Company https://f.hubspotusercontent40.net/hubfs/481991/Relocalizing%20Health%20Book/Split%20chapters%20and%20Case%20studies/Split%20case%20studies/Copper%20State%20Bolt%20&%20Nut%20Company.pdf
- Enovation Controls https://f.hubspotusercontent40.net/hubfs/481991/Relocalizing%20Health%20Book/Split%20chapters%20and%20Case%20studies/Split%20case%20studies/Enovation%20Controls.pdf
- ETEX Telephone Co-Operative https://f.hubspotusercontent40.net/hubfs/481991/Relocalizing%20Health%20Book/Split%20chapters%20and%20Case%20studies/Split%20case%20studies/ETEX%20Telephone%20Co-Operative.pdf
- Gasparilla Inn & Club https://f.hubspotusercontent40.net/hubfs/481991/Relocalizing%20Health%20Book/Split%20chapters%20and%20Case%20studies/Split%20case%20studies/Gasparilla%20Inn%20&%20Club.pdf
- Great Lakes Auto Network https://f.hubspotusercontent40.net/hubfs/481991/Relocalizing%20Health%20Book/Split%20chapters%20and%20Case%20studies/Split%20case%20studies/Great%20Lakes%20Auto%20Network.pdf
- Keystone Technologies https://f.hubspotusercontent40.net/hubfs/481991/Relocalizing%20Health%20Book/Split%20chapters%20and%20Case%20studies/Split%20case%20studies/Keystone%20Technologies.pdf

- Langdale Industries https://f.hubspotusercontent40.net/hubfs/481991/Relocalizing%20Health%20Book/Split%20chapters%20and%20Case%20studies/Split%20case%20studies/Langdale%20Industries.pdf
- Pacific Steel & Recycling https://f.hubspotusercontent40.net/hubfs/481991/Relocalizing%20Health%20Book/Split%20chapters%20and%20Case%20studies/Split%20case%20studies/Pacific%20Steel%20&%20Recycling.pdf
- Pittsburgh (Allegheny County) Schools https://f.hubspotusercontent40.net/hubfs/481991/Relocalizing%20Health%20Book/Split%20chapters%20and%20Case%20studies/Split%20case%20studies/Pittsburgh%20(Allegheny%20County)%20Schools.pdf
- Rosen Hotels & Resorts https://f.hubspotusercontent40.net/hubfs/481991/Relocalizing%20Health%20Book/Split%20chapters%20and%20Case%20studies/Split%20case%20studies/Rosen%20Hotels%20&%20Resorts.pdf
- Textum https://f.hubspotusercontent40.net/hubfs/481991/Relocalizing%20Health%20Book/Split%20chapters%20and%20Case%20studies/Split%20case%20studies/Textum.pdf

Also see Health Rosetta employer-led webinar page for more information about reducing medical care costs, https://members.healthrosetta.org/employer-webinars/#empintro.

Notes

Chapter 1

1. SingleCare Team (2021).
2. U.S. News & World Report (2021).
3. Harvard (2019).
4. Author's estimate base on the 2019 national health care expenditures of $3.8 trillion (n.d.).
5. Drillinger (2021).
6. Phone interview with Dr. Glenn Gero (2021).
7. Vlaev, King, Darzi, and Dolan (n.d.).
8. Pasichnyk (n.d.).
9. Ibid.
10. Ibid.
11. Aldana (2022a).
12. University of Wisconsin Population Health Institute (n.d).
13. Ibid.
14. See the Wellsteps.com blog for essays about these topics.
15. Aldana (2022b).
16. Hurst (2020).
17. Ibid.
18. Click on Detroit (2021).
19. U.S. Department of Agriculture (2020).
20. Ibid.
21. Ibid.
22. Harvard (2021).
23. Doheny (2020).
24. Gould (2020).
25. Ibid.
26. Perlmutter (n.d.).
27. Murphy (2021).
28. Robinson, Segal, and Smith (2021).

29. Geisinger (2021).

30. www.imdb.com/video/vi3172843033?playlistId=tt0057193&ref_=tt_ov_vi

Chapter 2

1. O'Neill (2022).

2. CDC, Covid Data Tracker (n.d.).

3. Vilet (2020). This essay was published in the first year of the pandemic discussing how more lives could have been saved with early outpatient treatments.

4. McCulla (2016).

5. Ibid.

6. Ibid.

7. Higgins (2020).

8. Devine (2017).

9. Ibid.

10. Ibid.

11. Steinrich (2020). According to Steinreich, "Eclectics emphasized plant remedies, bed rest, and steam baths, while homeopaths emphasized a different set of medicines in small doses (letting the body heal itself as much as possible), improved diet and hygiene, and stress reduction. The worst results these treatments produced were allergic reactions to no improvement. Hence it's not surprising they began to be preferred over the ghastly bleeding and metal injections of allopathy, which killed large numbers of patients."

12. Ibid.

13. Ibid. As Steinreich points out, "… doctors were firmly in the lower middle class at the time of the AMA's founding and made about $600 per year. This rose to about $1,000 around 1900. After Flexner, incomes began to skyrocket such that a 1928 AMA study found average annual incomes had reached a whopping (for the time) $6,354. Even during the Great Depression, physicians earned four times what average workers did. A 2009 survey put family practice doctors (on the low end of the physician income range) at a median of $197,655 and spine surgeons (at the high end) at a median of

$641,728. These figures are mind-boggling to ordinary Americans, even in good economic times. In addition, the cyclical unemployment that throws workers out of jobs in almost all other industries with the arrival of recessions or depressions became nonexistent among physicians after Flexner."

14. Accad (2016).
15. Steinreich (2020).
16. Vardy (2018).
17. Beito (2000), p. 109.
18. Ibid. pp. 109–110.
19. Ibid. 1113ff.
20. Ibid. 124 ff.

Chapter 3

1. Blue Facts (2021).
2. Ibid.
3. Ibid.
4. Ibid.
5. Thomasson (2003).
6. Gordon (2018).
7. Thomasson (2003).
8. Ibid.
9. Gordon (2018).
10. Thomasson (2003).
11. Ibid.
12. Ibid.
13. Communications Division of the Blue Cross and Blue Shield Association (n.d.).
14. BlueCross BlueShield. (n.d.).
15. Ibid.
16. Ibid.
17. BlueCross BlueShield (n.d.).
18. Ibid.
19. Ibid.

Chapter 4

1. Reed (1965).
2. Morrisey (2020), pp. 3–4.
3. Ibid. p. 8.
4. Ibid. p. 9.
5. Keisler-Starkey and Bunch (2021), p. 4.
6. Ibid.
7. Morrisey (2020), pp. 16–17.
8. For an overview of HMOs, PPOs, and POS plans, see Morrisey (2020) pp. 17–19.
9. KFF (2020), p. 2; Morrisey (2020), p. 19.
10. KFF (2020), p. 1. See this report for more data about the cost sharing for single employees and family plans, and how these costs vary by the size of the business.
11. Morrisey (2020), p. 20.
12. Rothbard (2017), *The Progressive Era,* for how the intellectual foundation of statism led to encroaching government regulations of major economic sectors. Not surprisingly, businesses at times were at the forefront of advocating more regulation in what has been described crony capitalism or regulatory capture.
13. Holly (2017).
14. KFF (2021).
15. UnitedHealth Group (n.d.).
16. Cigna (n.d.-b).
17. Cigna (n.d.-d).
18. Cigna (n.d.-c).
19. Humana (n.d.-a).
20. Humana (n.d.-b).
21. Humana (n.d.-c).
22. Aetna (n.d.-b).
23. Aetna (n.d.-a).
24. healthinsurance.org (n.d.).
25. Norris (2021).
26. healthinsurance.org (n.d.).

27. Ibid.

28. Himber (2021).

29. Ibid.

30. Ibid.

Chapter 5

1. Smith (2021).

2. Ibid.

3. Ibid.

4. Warren (n.d).

5. PeopleKeep® (n.d.).

6. Ibid.

7. PeopleKeep® (n.d.).

8. Ibid.

9. PeopleKeep® (2012).

10. Mayo Clinic (2021).

11. PeopleKeep® (2012).

12. Smith (2021).

13. PeopleKeep® (2012) and Cigna (n.d.-a).

14. Miller (2021).

15. Health Matching Account Services, Inc. (n.d.).

16. Health Matching Account Services, Inc. (n.d.).

Chapter 6

1. Bliss (n.d).

2. Ibid.

3. Rose (2020).

4. Ibid.

5. Ibid.

6. Favini (2021).

7. Forward (n.d.).

8. Ibid.

9. Forward (n.d.).

10. Optimum Direct Care (2019).

11. Hoff (2018).

11. Lehmann (2020).

Chapter 7

1. Daily (2019),

2. Dedication Health (n.d.).

3. Concierge Medicine Today (n.d.).

4. WebMD Editorial Contributors (2021).

5. Sullivan (2018).

6. Ibid.

Chapter 8

1. Beito (2000), p. 1.

2. Ibid. p. 3.

3. Ibid. p. 4.

4. Ibid. p. 45.

5. Ibid. pp. 109–111.

6. See Beito's illumining discussion regarding the debate over compulsory health insurance, pp. 142–160.

7. Beito (n.d.), pp. 161–180.

8. Healthsharing Reviews (2020).

9. Walker (2021).

10. Ibid.

11. Ibid.

Chapter 9

1. Yang (2021).

2. Shmerling (2021).

3. Ibid.

4. Ibid.

5. Ibid.

6. Ibid.

7. Ibid.

8. Galvin (2021).

9. Kearney, Montero, Hamel, and Brodie (2021).

10. St. Onge (2020).

11. Allin, Marchildon, and Peckham (2020).

12. Ibid.

13. St. Onge (2020).

14. Kurisko (2009).

15. Thorlby (2020).

16. Ibid.

17. Ibid.

18. Ibid.

19. Evans (2019).

20. Ibid.

21. Ibid.

22. Tsung-Mei (2020).

23. Ibid.

24. Ibid.

25. Ibid.

26. Ibid.

27. Ibid.

28. Siok (2018).

29. Ibid.

30. Norris (2021).

31. AARP Medicare Plans (n.d.).

32. Einhorn (2019).

33. Ibid.

34. Ibid.

35. Ibid.

36. Pham (2019).

37. International Insurance.com (n.d.).

38. The Borgen Project (2020).

39. Ibid.

40. Sturny (2020).

41. Lee (2020).

42. Blümel and Busse (2020).

43. Ibid.

Chapter 10

1. Being and staying healthy is ultimately our responsibility. Wellness has more to do with lifestyle choices than traditional medical practices. Sabrin (2021).

2. Safavi, Stephan, McCaghy, Brombach, and Rao (2018). The goal of this chapter is to demonstrate that the "system" is not patient-friendly and thus patients would be better served with a new medical care paradigm.

3. Bennett, Jr. (2019).

4. Ibid.

5. Ibid.

6. Ibid.

7. FMMA, "About US."

8. FMMA, "Pillars of the FMMA."

9. Smith (2021).

10. Ibid.

11. O'Brien (2021).

12. Ibid.

13. Yang (2021).

14. Spenser James Group (n.d.).

15. Self-Insurance Institute of America, Inc. (n.d.).

16. Ibid.

17. Ibid.

18. Ibid.

19. Ibid.

20. Enthoven (2021).

21. Ibid.

22. Ibid.

23. Ibid.

24. Ibid.

25. ValuePenguin (2021).

26. Caldwell (2021).

27. Allen (2018).

28. Health Rosetta (n.d.-b).

29. Health Rosetta (n.d.-a).

30. Ibid.
31. Chase (n.d.).
32. MPBHealth® (n.d.).
33. Ibid.

References

AARP Medicare Plans. n.d. "Is Medicare Mandatory?" www.aarpmedicareplans
.com/medicare-articles/is-medicare-mandatory.html (accessed November 01,
2021).

Accad. M. May 24, 2016. "The Early History of Regulated Health Care." *Ludwig
von Mises Institute.* https://mises.org/wire/early-history-regulated-health-care.

Aetna. n.d.-a. "Get the Best of Both Worlds With Aetna EPO." www.aetna.com/
health-insurance-plans/epo.html (accessed October 30, 2021).

Aetna. n.d. "Our history." www.aetna.com/about-us/aetna-history.html (accessed
October 30, 2021).

Aldana, S. February 02, 2022. "18 Wellness Program Incentive Ideas From
the Best Corporate Wellness Programs." *WellSteps.* www.wellsteps.com/
blog/2020/01/02/wellness-program-incentive-ideas/.

Aldana, S. March 01, 2022. "14 Reasons Many Corporate Health and
Wellness Programs Fail 2022 Update." Wellsteps. www.wellsteps.com/
blog/2020/01/02/corporate-health-and-wellness-programs/.

Allen, M. October 18, 2018. "In Montana, A Tough Negotiator Proved Employers
Don't Have to Pay So Much for Health Care." *ProPublica.* www.propublica.org/
article/in-montana-a-tough-negotiator-proved-employers-do-not-have-to-
pay-so-much-for-health-care?utm_campaign=Relocalizing%20Health%20
Launch&utm_medium=email&_hsmi=97773450&_hsenc=p2ANqtz-
8ueJqpyW1KEPo5E7RshpCYcOCgHa7h6MrH6eGOwelA5o7x7za
9g_s1QGIugQhF3HARoOSKUixcnmdgUCade1Dhfy1EVQ&utm_
content=97773450&utm_source=hs_automation.

Allin, S., G. Marchildon, and A. Peckham. June 5, 2020. *Canada,* The
Commonwealth Fund. https://www.commonwealthfund.org/international-
health-policy-center/countries/canada.

Author's estimate base on the 2019 national health care expenditures of $3.8
trillion. n.d. www.cms.gov/Research-Statistics-Data-and-Systems/Statistics-
Trends-and-Reports/NationalHealthExpendData/NHE-Fact-Sheet.

Beito, D. 2000. *From Mutual Aid to the Welfare State: Fraternal Societies and Social
Services, 189-1967.* Chapel Hill: The University of North Carolina Press.

Bennett, W., Jr. October 22, 2019. "Insurance Companies Aren't Doctors. So
Why Do We Keep Letting Them Practice Medicine?" *The Washington Post.*
www.washingtonpost.com/opinions/2019/10/22/insurance-companies-
arent-doctors-so-why-do-we-keep-letting-them-practice-medicine/.

Bliss. G. n.d. "The Origins of Direct Primary Care: Transformation, Simple Ideas, and Trojan Horse." *Hint Health.* https://blog.hint.com/direct-primary-care-origins.

Bliss. G. n.d. "The Origins of Direct Primary Care: Transformation, Simple Ideas, and Trojan Horse." *hint health.* https://blog.hint.com/direct-primary-care-origins.

Blue Cross Blue Shield Association. n.d."Healthcare Coverage Design for Your Community, Accessible Across the Country." www.bcbs.com/sites/default/files/file-attachments/page/Blue_Facts_Sheet-2021.pdf (accessed September 25, 2021).

BlueCross BlueShield. n.d. "Improving Care, Nationwide." www.bcbs.com/improving-care-nationwide (accessed September 25, 2021).

BlueCross BlueShield. n.d. "Leading the Way Toward a Future Where Data Empowers Patients." www.bcbs.com/the-health-of-america/articles/leading-the-way-toward-future-where-data-empowers-patients (accessed September 25, 2021).

Blümel, M. and R. Busse. June 05, 2020. The Commonwealth Fund. Germany. www.commonwealthfund.org/international-health-policy-center/countries/germany.

Caldwell, M. December 14, 2021. "Traditional Health Insurance Plan vs. High–Deductible Plan: What's The Difference?" The balance. www.thebalance.com/traditional-vs-high-deductible-health-insurance-2385891.

CDC. n.d. "COVID Data Tracker." https://covid.cdc.gov/covid-data-tracker/#datatracker-home (accessed March 04, 2022).

Chase, D. n.d., *The CEO's Guide to Restoring the American Dream: How to Deliver World Class Health Care to Your Employees at Half the Cost.* Executive Summary, getabstract. https://members.healthrosetta.org/wp-content/uploads/2020/07/The-CEOs-Guide-to-Restoring-the-American-Dream-Exec-sum.pdf.

Cigna®. n.d.-a. "Cigna Flexible Savings Accounts." Accessed September 27, 2021. www.cigna.com/employers-brokers/savings-spending-accounts/fsa.

Cigna®. n.d.-b. "Cigna Milestones." www.cigna.com/about-us/company-profile/milestones (accessed September 27, 2021).

Cigna®. n.d.-c. "Controlling Costs and Improving Quality." www.cigna.com/employers-brokers/why-cigna/plans-networks (accessed September 27, 2021).

Cigna®. n.d.-d. "Six Simple Reasons to Partner With Us." www.cigna.com/employers-brokers/why-cigna/ (accessed September 27, 2021).

Communications Division of the Blue Cross and Blue Shield Association. n.d. "BCBSA History Fact Sheet." https://digitalcommons.unf.edu/cgi/viewcontent.cgi?article=3089&context=flablue_text (accessed September 25, 2021).

Concierge Medicine Today. n.d. "The History of Concierge Medicine in America (1996-Present Day)." https://conciergemedicinetoday.org/the-history-of-concierge-medicine-in-america-1996-present-day/ (accessed October 29, 2021).

Daily, L. October 22, 2019. "Before You Pay Extra to Join a Concierge Medical Practice, Consider These Questions." *Washington Post.* www.washingtonpost.com/lifestyle/home/before-you-pay-extra-to-join-a-concierge-medical-practice-consider-these-questions/2019/10/21/90d8206a-ef8b-11e9-b648-76bcf86eb67e_story.html.

Dedication Health. n.d. "Why Employers Should Consider Concierge Medicine for Employees." www.dedication-health.com/why-employers-should-consider-concierge-medicine-for-employees/ (accessed October 29, 2021).

Devine, S. July 06, 2017. "Healthcare and the American medical profession 1830–1880." www.journalofthecivilwarera.org/2017/07/health-care-american-medical-profession-1830-1880/.

Doheny, K. January 02, 2020. "Mediterranean Diet Repeats as Best Overall of 2020." *WebMd.* www.webmd.com/diet/news/20200102/mediterranean-diet-repeats-as-best-overall-of-2020.

Drillinger, M. March 21, 2021. "42% of Americans Said They Gained Weight During the Pandemic." *Healthline.* www.healthline.com/health-news/61-percent-of-americans-say-they-gained-weight-during-the-pandemic.

Einhorn, E.S. February 25, 2019. "Healthcare in the Nordics." *nordicsinfo.* https://nordics.info/show/artikel/healthcare-in-the-nordic-region/.

Enthoven, A.C. August 13, 2021. "Employer Self-Funded Health Insurance Is Taking Us In The Wrong Direction." *Health Affairs.* www.healthaffairs.org/do/10.1377/forefront.20210811.56839.

Evans, T. May 03, 2019. "London Calling: Don't Commit to Nationalized Health Care." *The Heritage Foundation.* www.heritage.org/sites/default/files/2019-05/BG3405.pdf.

Favini, N. March 12, 2021. "How I Realized that Healthcare is Backwards." *Forward.* https://goforward.com/blog/healthcare-is-backwards/how-i-realized-that-healthcare-is-backwards.

Flynn, S.M. 2019. *The Cure That Works: How to Have the World's Best Healthcare—at a Quarter of the Price.* Washington DC: Regnery Publishing.

FMMA. n.d. "About Us." https://fmma.org/about-us/ (accessed January 15, 2022).

FMMA. n.d. "Pillars of the FMMA." https://fmma.org/pillars/ (accessed January 15, 2022).

Forward. n.d. "A world Where Everyone Has Access to Best Medical Care Available." https://goforward.com/about-us (accessed October 04, 2021).

Forward. n.d. "Healthcare vs. Sickcare: Why Only Seeing a Doctor When You Need One is Totally Backwards." https://blog.goforward.com/healthcare-is-backwards/healthcare-vs-sickcare (accessed October 04, 2021).

Galvin, G. March 24, 2021. "About 7 in 10 Voters Favor a Public Health Insurance Option. Medicare for All Remains Polarizing." *Morning Consult*®. https://morningconsult.com/2021/03/24/medicare-for-all-public-option-polling/.

Gordon, J.S. 2018. "A Short History of American Medical Insurance." *Imprimis* 47. no. 9. https://imprimis.hillsdale.edu/short-history-american-medical-insurance/.

Gould, H. November 19, 2020. "10 popular diets that actually work." *Byrdie*. www.byrdie.com/popular-diets-that-work-5080746.

Harvard, T.H. December 18, 2019. "Close to Half of U.S. Population to Have Obesity by 2030." Cahn School of Public Health. www.hsph.harvard.edu/news/press-releases/half-of-us-to-have-obesity-by-2030/.

Harvard, T.H. January 12, 2021. "Dietary Guidelines for Americans released." Chan School of Public Health. www.hsph.harvard.edu/nutritionsource/2021/01/12/2020-dietary-guidelines/.

Health Matching Account Services, Inc. n.d. "HMA® Account Balance Growth Explosion." www.healthmatchingaccounts.com/hma-account-balance-growth-explanation/ (accessed October 11, 2021).

Health Matching Account Services, Inc. n.d. "HMA® FAQ." www.healthmatchingaccounts.com/hma-faq/ (accessed October 11, 2021).

Health Rosetta. n.d.-a. "Employers." https://healthrosetta.org/employers/ (accessed February 17, 2022).

Health Rosetta. n.d.-b. "Our Mission." https://healthrosetta.org/mission/ (accessed February 17, 2022).

Healthinsurance.org.™ n.d. "Individual Health Insurance." www.healthinsurance.org/glossary/individual-health-insurance/ (accessed October 11, 2021).

Healthsharing Reviews. March 05, 2020. "What is a Shared Health Network." December 02, 2021. https://healthsharingreviews.com/what-is-a-shared-health-network/.

Higgins, K. April 01, 2020. "Lessons From a Revolutionary Epidemic." The American Revolution Institute. www.americanrevolutioninstitute.org/lessons-from-a-revolutionary-epidemic/.

Himber, V. September 22, 2021. "Definition of Group Heath Insurance." *ehealth*®. www.ehealthinsurance.com/resources/small-business/definition-of-group-health-insurance.

Hoff, T. September 06, 2018. "Direct Primary Care Has Limited Benefits for Doctors and Patients." STAT. www.statnews.com/2018/09/06/direct-primary-care-doctors-patients/.

Holly, M. May 05, 2017 "How Government Regulations Made Healthcare So Expensive." *Ludwig von Mises Institute.* https://mises.org/wire/how-government-regulations-made-healthcare-so-expensive.

Humana. n.d.-a. "About Humana." www.humana.com/about/ (accessed September 28, 2021).

Humana. n.d.-b. "Small Business and Large Group Medical Insurance." www .humana.com/employer/products-services/medical-plans (accessed September 28, 2021).

Humana. n.d.-c. "The Go365 Five-Year Study." https://docushare-web.apps .external.pioneer.humana.com/Marketing/docushare-app?file=2853084 (accessed September 28, 2021).

Hurst, A. March 24, 2020. "Americans Aren't Doing Enough to Stay Healthy." www.valuepenguin.com/unhealthiest-habits-in-america.

International Insurance.com. n.d. "Understanding Health Insurance in Switzerland." www.internationalinsurance.com/health/europe/switzerland .php (accessed January 05, 2021).

Kearney, A., A. Montero, L. Hamel, and M. Brodie. December 14, 2021. "Americans' Challenges with Health Care Costs." *KFF.* www.kff.org/health-costs/issue-brief/americans-challenges-with-health-care-costs/.

KFF. February 04, 2021. "Surprise Medical Bills: New Protections for Consumers Take Effect in 2022." www.kff.org/private-insurance/fact-sheet/surprise-medical-bills-new-protections-for-consumers-take-effect-in-2022/ (accessed November 2021).

KFF. October 2020. "2020 Employer Health Benefits Survey." www.kff.org/ report-section/ehbs-2020-summary-of-findings/ (accessed November 2021).

Kurisko, L. 2009. *Health Reform: The End of the American Revolution?* St. Paul. MN: Alethos Press LLC.

Lee, C.E. June 06, 2020. Singapore: The Commonwealth Fund. www.common wealthfund.org/international-health-policy-center/countries/singapore.

Lehmann, C. February 06, 2020. "More Patients Turning to 'Direct Primary Care'." WebMD®. www.webmd.com/health-insurance/news/20200206/more-patients-turning-to-direct-primary-care.

Mayo Clinic. March 25, 2021. "Health savings account: Is an HSA right for you?" www.mayoclinic.org/healthy-lifestyle/consumer-health/in-depth/health-savings-accounts/art-20044058 (accessed December 06, 2021).

McCulla, T. 2016. "Medicine in Colonial America." Colonial North America as Harvard Library. https://colonialnorthamerica.library.harvard.edu/spotlight/ cna/feature/medicine-in-colonial-north-america.

Miller, S. November 11, 2021. "2022 Health FSA Contribution Cap Rises to $2850." *SHRM®.* www.shrm.org/resourcesandtools/hr-topics/benefits/ pages/2022-fsa-contribution-cap-and-other-colas.aspx.

MPBHealth®. n.d. "Groups." https://mpb.health/groups/ (accessed February 18, 2022).

Murphy, J. September 04, 2021. "Four Exercise Routines to Help You Stay in Shape This Fall." *The Wall Street Journal.* www.wsj.com/articles/exercise-routines-fall-11630607199.

N.A. February 25, 2021. "Here Is One Laughter Is the Best Medicine." Geisinger. www.geisinger.org/health-and-wellness/wellness-articles/2021/02/25/19/56/why-laughter-is-the-best-medicine.

Norris, L. December 08, 2021. "Is There Still a Penalty for Being Uninsured in 2021?" *verywellheatlh.* www.verywellhealth.com/obamacare-penalty-for-being-uninsured-4132434.

Norris, L. July 21, 2021. "Obamacare's Essential Health Benefits." Healthinsurance .org™. www.healthinsurance.org/obamacare/essential-health-benefits/.

O'Brien. S. November 11. 2021. "Average Family Premiums for Employer-Based Health Insurance Have Jumped 47% in the Last Decade, Outpacing Wage Growth and Inflation." *CNBC.* www.cnbc.com/2021/11/11/premiums-for-employer-health-insurance-have-jumped-47percent-in-10-years.html.

O'Neill, A. February 02, 2022. "United States Life Expectancy at Birth From 2009-2019." *Statista.* www.statista.com/statistics/263724/life-expectancy-in-the-united-states/.

Optimum Direct Care. July 26, 2019. "Direct Primary Care Statistics." https://optimumdirectcare.com/direct-primary-care-statistics/ (accessed November 10, 2021).

PeopleKeep®. May 15, 2012. "History of Health Savings Account—MSAs to HSAs." www.peoplekeep.com/blog/bid/143476/history-of-health-savings-accounts-msas-to-hsas (accessed October 27, 2021).

PeopleKeep®. May 16, 2012. "History of Flexible Savings Accounts." www .peoplekeep.com/blog/bid/143464/history-of-flexible-spending-accounts-fsas (accessed October 27, 2021).

PeopleKeep®. n.d. "Individual coverage HRA (ICHRA)." www.peoplekeep.com/individual-coverage-hra-ichra (accessed October 27, 2021).

PeopleKeep®. n.d. "Qualified Small Employer HRA (QSEHRA)." www .peoplekeep.com/qualified-small-employer-hra-qsehra (accessed October 27, 2021).

Perlmutter. D. n.d. "Low-Carb." *davidperlmutter MD.* www.drperlmutter.com/focus-area/low-carb/.

Pham, K. June 13, 2019. "'Socialist' Nordic Countries Are Actually Moving Toward Private Health Care." *The Heritage Foundation.* www.heritage.org/health-care-reform/commentary/socialist-nordic-countries-are-actually-moving-toward-private-health.

Reed, L.S. December 1965. "Private Health Insurance in the United States: An Overview." *Bulletin.* www.ssa.gov/policy/docs/ssb/v28n12/v28n12p3.pdf.

Robinson, L., J. Segal, and M. Smith. August 2021. "The Mental Health Benefits of Exercise." *HelpGuide.* www.helpguide.org/articles/healthy-living/the-mental-health-benefits-of-exercise.htm.

Rose, A. June 23, 2020. "Direct Primary Care: Physicians Share Their Pros and Cons." *DDW.* www.healthecareers.com/ddw/article/career/direct-primary-care-physicians-share-their-pros-and-cons?gclid=Cj0KCQiAtJeNBhCVARIsANJ UJ2FeR3eXq-tlTb7j9iw6HKupBIL2A1VpK2a-fEzYx-kundI62qebuvEaAn-6uEALw_wcB.

Rothbard, M.N. 2017. *The Progressive Era.* Auburn: AL. Ludwig von Mises Institute.

Sabrin, M. 2021. *Universal Medical Care From Conception To End-Of-Life: The Case For Single-Payer System.* Page Publishing: Conneaut Lake, PA.

Safavi, K., J.P. Stephan, L. McCaghy, M. Brombach, and S. Rao. November 06, 2018. "U.S. Health Plans Can Save Billions by Helping Patients Navigate the System." *Harvard Business Review.* https://hbr.org/2018/11/u-s-health-plans-can-save-billions-by-helping-patients-navigate-the-system.

Schneider, E., A. Shah, M.M. Doty, R. Tikkanen, K. Fields, and R.D. Williams II. August 04, 2021. *Mirror, Mirror 2021: Reflecting Poorly: Health Care in the U.S. Compared to Other High-Income Countries.* The Commonwealth Fund. www.commonwealthfund.org/publications/fund-reports/2021/aug/mirror-mirror-2021-reflecting-poorly.

Self-Insurance Institute of America, Inc. n.d. "Self Insured Group Health Plans." www.siia.org/i4a/pages/index.cfm?pageid=7533 (accessed February 15, 2022).

SingleCare Team. January 21, 2021. "Overweight and Obesity Statistics 2021." U.S. www.singlecare.com/blog/news/obesity-statistics/ (accessed September 14, 2021).

Siok, H.L. November 13, 2018. "Health Care for All: The Good and Not-So-Great of Taiwan's Universal Coverage." *The News Lens.* https://international .thenewslens.com/article/108032.

Shmerling, R.H. July 13, 2021. "Is Our Healthcare System Broken?" *Harvard Health Publishing.* www.health.harvard.edu/blog/is-our-healthcare-system-broken-202107132542.

Smith, G. October 17, 2021. "HSA vs. HRA: Should I Offer One, the Other, or Both?" *PeopleKeep®.* www.peoplekeep.com/blog/should-i-offer-an-hra-an-hsa-or-both.

Smith, K. 2021. Surgery Center of Oklahoma. https://surgerycenterok.com/ blog-category/dr-keith-smith-at-the-2021-medical-freedom-summit/ (accessed January 16, 2022).

Spenser James Group. n.d. "Why Is Self Insurance Gaining Popularity for Business." www.spencerjamesgroup.com/blog/self-insurance-for-businesses (accessed February 14, 2022).

St. Onge, P. February 20, 2020. "How Socialized Medicine Hurts Canadians and Leaves Them Worse Off Financially." *The Heritage Foundation.* www.heritage.org/health-care-reform/report/how-socialized-medicine-hurts-canadians-and-leaves-them-worse-financially.

Steinreich. D. September 22, 2020. "100 Years of Medical Fascism." *Ludwig von Mises Institute.* https://mises.org/library/one-hundred-years-medical-fascism.

Sturny, I. June 5, 2020. Switzerland: The Commonwealth Fund. www.commonwealthfund.org/international-health-policy-center/countries/switzerland.

Sullivan, P. April 20, 2018. "An E.R. That Treats You Like a V.I.P." *The New York Times.* www.nytimes.com/2018/04/20/your-money/concierge-emergency-room.html?searchResultPosition=4.

The Borgen Project. 2020. "An Overview of Healthcare In Switzerland." https://borgenproject.org/healthcare-in-switzerland/ (accessed January 10, 2022).

Thomasson, M. April 17, 2003. "Health Insurance in the United States". EH.Net Encyclopedia, edited by R. Whaples. http://eh.net/encyclopedia/health-insurance-in-the-united-states/.

Thorlby, R. June 05, 2020. England: The Commonwealth Fund. www.commonwealthfund.org/international-health-policy-center/countries/england.

Tsung-Mei, C. May 02, 2020. "A Lesson for AMERICA: Taiwan's Single-Payer National Health Insurance." *Milken Institute Review.* www.milkenreview.org/articles/a-lesson-for-america.

U.S. News & World Report. March 24, 2021. "Obesity Costs the Average U.S. Adult Almost $1,900 per Year: Study." www.usnews.com/news/health-news/articles/2021-03-24/obesity-costs-the-average-us-adult-almost-1-900-per-year-study.

UnitedHealth Group®. n.d. "Improving HealthCare Affordability." https://sustainability.uhg.com/modernizing-health-care/improving-affordability.html (accessed October 15, 2021).

University of Wisconsin Population Health Institute. n.d. "Financial Rewards for a Employee Healthy Behavior." www.countyhealthrankings.org/take-action-to-improve-health/what-works-for-health/strategies/financial-rewards-for-employee-healthy-behavior (accessed September 16, 2021).

U.S. Department of Agriculture. 2020. "Dietary Guidelines for Americans: 2020-2025." www.dietaryguidelines.gov/sites/default/files/2020-12/Dietary_Guidelines_for_Americans_2020-2025.pdf (accessed September 10, 2021).

ValuePenguin. 2021. "Largest Insurance Companies of 2022." www
.valuepenguin.com/largest-health-insurance-companies#member (accessed
February 15, 2022).

Vardy. N. November 20, 2018. "Is Warren Buffett the Ultimate Anti-Capitalist."
Liberty Through Wealth. https://libertythroughwealth.com/2018/11/20/
warren-buffett-anti-capitalist-anti-competition/.

Vlaev, I., D. King, A. Darzi, and P. Dolan. 2019. "Changing Health Behaviors
Using Financial Incentives: A Review From Behavioral Economics." *BMC
Public Health* 19, p. 1059. https://doi.org/10.1186/s12889-019-7407-8.

Walker, E. November 19, 2021. "Pros & Cons of Healthcare Sharing Ministries."
PeopleKeep®. www.peoplekeep.com/blog/pros-and-cons-of-healthcare-sharing-
ministries.

Warren, H. n.d. "What Is Essential Minimum Coverage (MEC)?" *PeopleKeep®*.
https://peoplekeephelp.zendesk.com/hc/en-us/articles/360035075914-
What-is-minimum-essential-coverage-MEC-#:~:text=Minimum%20
essential%20coverage%20(MEC)%20refers,the%2010%20essential%20
health%20benefits.

WebMD®. June 29, 2021. "What Is a Concierge Doctor." WebMD Editorial
Contributors. www.webmd.com/a-to-z-guides/what-is-a-concierge-doctor
(accessed November 25, 2021).

www.imdb.com/video/vi3172843033?playlistId=tt0057193&ref_=tt_ov_vi

Yang, J. November 11, 2021. "Percentage of U.S. Workers Covered by Self-
Funded Health Insurance Plans From 1999 to 2021." *Statista*. www.statista
.com/statistics/985324/self-funded-health-insurance-covered-workers/.

Yang, J. November 26, 2021. "Percentage of Respondents Worldwide Who
Were Satisfied With Their Country's National Health System as of 2019, by
Country." *Statista*. www.statista.com/statistics/1109036/satisfaction-health-
system-worldwide-by-country/.

About the Author

Dr. Murray Sabrin joined the faculty of the Anisfield School of Business of Ramapo College of New Jersey in 1985 and retired on July 1, 2020, as Professor of Finance. Over the course of his career, he taught several courses including Corporate Finance, Securities and Investments, and Financial History of the United States. On January 25, 2021, the board of trustees awarded Dr. Sabrin Emeritus status for his scholarship and professional contributions during his 35-year career.

In 2007, the Sabrins made a $250,000 gift to Ramapo College to establish the Sabrin Center for Free Enterprise in the Anisfield School of Business (www.ramapo.edu/sabrincenter), and they made a $50,000 donation to establish the Sabrin Center study room in the Peter F. Mercer Learning Commons that opened in the fall of 2021.

Dr. Sabrin is considered a "public intellectual" as he has written essays about the economy for *The Record*, *Star-Ledger*, *Trenton Times*, and the *Asbury Park Press*. He has been a frequent guest on local, regional, and national talk radio shows and on national and international podcasts. His essays have also appeared in *Commerce Magazine*, *Mid-Atlantic Journal of Business*, *Nonprofit Management & Leadership, Indian Management*, and *Privatization Review* among other scholarly and popular publications.

Recently, Dr. Sabrin's book, *Universal Medical Care: From Conception to End-of-Life: The Case for a Single Payer System* (2021), outlined his vision for medical care, where the individual or family is in charge of their medical decisions. The "individual" single-payer system is based on restoring the doctor–patient relationship as well as other reforms. Also in 2021, Sabrin's *Navigating the Boom/Bust Cycle: An Entrepreneur's Survival Guide* was published by Business Expert Press.

Sabrin is the author of *Tax Free 2000: The Rebirth of American Liberty*, a blueprint to create a tax-free America in the 21st century, and *Why the Federal Reserve Sucks: It Causes Inflation, Recessions, Bubbles and Enriches the One Percent*, which is available on Amazon. His commentary about the economy and public policy is available at murraysabrin.substack.com.

In 2003, Dr. Sabrin was invited to serve as a founding trustee of the Bergen Volunteer Medical Initiative (BVMI) located in Hackensack, New Jersey, where he served until 2008.

Murray Sabrin arrived in America from West Germany at the age of two with his parents and older brother on August 6, 1949, and became a U.S. citizen in June 1959. His parents were the only members of their respective families to survive the Holocaust. The Sabrin family moved from the Lower East Side of Manhattan to the Bronx in 1953, and in 1968 Murray and his wife, Florence, were married. They moved to New Jersey in 1977 and relocated to Florida in 2021.

Dr. Sabrin graduated from the Bronx High School of Science in 1964. He has a BA in history, geography, and social studies education from Hunter College; an MA in social studies education from Lehman College; and a PhD in economic geography from Rutgers University. Sabrin is only one of the two individuals who had the honor of having the late Austrian school economist, historian, and philosopher Murray N. Rothbard serve as a member of his dissertation committee. His dissertation, "The Spatial Incidence of Inflation in the United States 1967–1971: An Economic-Geographic Perspective," was reviewed by a University of Chicago professor who stated, "You are to be congratulated on the theoretical and critical depth of your thesis."

In 1997, he was the New Jersey Libertarian Party's nominee for governor and made political history when he raised sufficient funds to participate in the state's matching fund program, which required him to participate in three debates with the two major party candidates. He also has sought the Republican nomination for the U.S. Senate.

Index

OTHER TITLES IN THE HEALTHCARE MANAGEMENT COLLECTION

Joy Field, Editor

- *Better Outcomes* by Rafael E. Salazar
- *Emergency Management for Healthcare, Volume IV* by Norman Ferrier
- *Emergency Management for Healthcare, Volume III* by Norman Ferrier
- *Emergency Management for Healthcare, Volume II* by Norman Ferrier
- *Emergency Management for Healthcare, Volume I* by Norman Ferrier
- *Strategic Data Management for Successful Healthcare Outcomes* by Lakkaraju Hema
- *Improv to Improve Healthcare* by Candy Campbell
- *Integrated Delivery* by David Stehlik
- *Mastering Evaluation and Management Services in Healthcare* by Stacy Swartz
- *Lean Thinking for Emerging Healthcare Leaders* by Arnout Orelio
- *Process-Oriented Healthcare Management Systems* by Anita Edvinsson
- *Behind the Scenes of Health Care* by Hesston L. Johnson
- *Predictive Medicine* by Emmanuel Fombu

Concise and Applied Business Books

The Collection listed above is one of 30 business subject collections that Business Expert Press has grown to make BEP a premiere publisher of print and digital books. Our concise and applied books are for...

- Professionals and Practitioners
- Faculty who adopt our books for courses
- Librarians who know that BEP's Digital Libraries are a unique way to offer students ebooks to download, not restricted with any digital rights management
- Executive Training Course Leaders
- Business Seminar Organizers

Business Expert Press books are for anyone who needs to dig deeper on business ideas, goals, and solutions to everyday problems. Whether one print book, one ebook, or buying a digital library of 110 ebooks, we remain the affordable and smart way to be business smart. For more information, please visit www.businessexpertpress.com, or contact sales@businessexpertpress.com.